WHAT IS THE GOSPEL OF MATTHEW?

Kids' Guides to God's Word Series

What Is the Book of Genesis?
What Is the Book of Exodus?
What Is the Book of Leviticus?
What Is the Book of Numbers?
What Is the Book of Deuteronomy?
What Is the Book of Joshua?
What Is the Book of Judges?
What Is the Book of Ruth?
What Is the Book of 1 Samuel?
What Is the Book of 2 Samuel?
What Is the Book of 1 Kings?
What Is the Book of 2 Kings?
What Are the Books of 1–2 Chronicles?
What Are the Books of Ezra & Nehemiah?
What Is the Book of Esther?
What Is the Book of Job?
What Is the Book of Psalms?
What Is the Book of Proverbs?
What Is the Book of Ecclesiastes?
What Are the Books of Song of Songs &
Lamentations?
What Is the Book of Isaiah?
What Is the Book of Jeremiah?
What Is the Book of Ezekiel?
What Is the Book of Daniel?
What Are the Books of Hosea–Micah?
What Are the Books of Nahum–Malachi?

What Is the Gospel of Matthew?
What Is the Gospel of Mark?
What Is the Gospel of Luke?
What Is the Gospel of John?
What Is the Book of Acts?
What Is the Book of Romans?
What Is the Book of 1 Corinthians?
What Is the Book of 2 Corinthians?
What Is the Book of Galatians?
What Is the Book of Ephesians?
What Is the Book of Philippians?
What Are the Books of Colossians
& Philemon?
What Are the Books of 1–2 Thessalonians?
What Are the Books of 1–2 Timothy & Titus?
What Is the Book of Hebrews?
What Is the Book of James?
What Are the Books of 1–2 Peter & Jude?
What Are the Books of 1-3 John?
What Is the Book of Revelation?

What Is the Gospel of
MATTHEW?

Michael Whitworth

ISBN 978-1-971767-15-4

Published by Start2Finish
Bend, Oregon 97702
start2finish.org

Printed in the United States of America
30 29 28 27 26   1 2 3 4 5

For my daughter Autumn—

May you always be captivated by the story of Jesus.
Daddy loves you.

CONTENTS

INTRODUCTION

Imagine you've been waiting for something your entire life. Not waiting like you wait for summer vacation or your birthday—though that feels long enough. I mean waiting the way your great-great-great-grandparents waited, and their great-great-great-grandparents before them. Imagine your family has been waiting for the same thing for hundreds of years. Imagine you've grown up hearing stories about a promise that was made before anyone you know was born—a promise that someone was coming who would change everything.

Now imagine the wait is finally over.

That's what the Gospel of Matthew is about. It's the announcement that the King has arrived.

THE LONG WAIT

To understand Matthew, you need to understand the wait. About two thousand years before Jesus was born, God made a promise to a man named Abraham: "Through your offspring, all nations on earth will be blessed." Abraham's descendants became the nation of Israel. They multiplied in Egypt, escaped through the Red Sea, wandered in the wilderness, and finally settled in a land God had promised them.

Then God made another promise—this time to King David. One of David's descendants would sit on the throne forever. His kingdom would never end.

But things didn't go according to plan. At least, not the plan Israel expected. The kingdom split in two. The people forgot God and worshiped idols. Prophets warned them to turn back, but they didn't listen. Eventually, enemies conquered them. The northern kingdom fell to Assyria. The southern kingdom fell to Babylon. The temple was destroyed. The people were dragged into exile. And just like that, David's throne sat empty.

When Israel finally returned to their land, they were never truly free again. The Persians ruled them. Then the Greeks. Then the Romans. Century after century, God's people lived under foreign occupation, clinging to the ancient promises: Someone is coming. A king from David's line. A Messiah. He will rescue us. He will restore the kingdom. He will make everything right.

By the time Jesus was born, Israel had been waiting for about six hundred years since the exile. Some people had given up hope. Others held on fiercely, scanning the horizon for any sign that deliverance was near.

And then, in a small town called Bethlehem, a baby was born.

WHY MATTHEW WROTE THIS BOOK

Matthew was one of Jesus' twelve disciples. Before Jesus called him, he worked as a tax collector—one of the most hated professions in Israel. Tax collectors worked for Rome, the occupying empire. They were seen as traitors, getting rich by squeezing money out of their own people. But Jesus called Matthew anyway. "Follow me," he said. And Matthew got up, left everything, and followed.

Years later, Matthew wrote this book. And he wrote it with a specific purpose: to prove that Jesus was the King Israel had been waiting for.

That's why Matthew begins with a genealogy—a family tree. It might seem like a boring way to start a book, but for Matthew's original readers, it was explosive. The genealogy traces Jesus' ancestry through David all the way back to Abraham. Matthew is saying: This is the one. The promised descendant of Abraham. The heir to David's throne. The Messiah.

Throughout his book, Matthew quotes the Old Testament more than any other Gospel writer. Again and again, he shows how Jesus fulfilled prophecies that were written centuries before he was born. Born in Bethlehem? Predicted. Raised in Nazareth? Predicted. Healing the sick? Predicted. Betrayed for thirty pieces of silver? Predicted. Even the way he died was written about hundreds of years in advance.

Matthew wants you to see the connections. He wants you to realize that Jesus didn't just show up randomly. His arrival was the climax of a story that had been building since the beginning of time.

WHAT YOU'RE ABOUT TO READ

Here's a roadmap of where we're headed:

The King Arrives (Chapters 1–4). Matthew introduces Jesus through his family tree, his miraculous birth, and the early events of his life—visited by wise men, escaping to Egypt, baptized by John, and tempted by Satan in the wilderness. By the end of chapter 4, Jesus has begun preaching his central message: "Repent, for the kingdom of heaven has come near."

The King's Manifesto (Chapters 5–7). This is the famous Sermon on the Mount, where Jesus describes what life in his kingdom looks like. Blessed are the poor in spirit. Love your enemies. Don't worry about tomorrow. Build your life on the rock. It's the most famous sermon ever preached, and it still challenges everyone who reads it.

The King's Power (Chapters 8–9). Jesus doesn't just talk—he acts. He heals lepers, calms storms, casts out demons, and even raises the dead. Each miracle demonstrates that the King has authority over sickness, nature, evil, and death itself.

The King's Mission and Opposition (Chapters 10–12). Jesus sends out his disciples to spread the message, but not everyone welcomes them. The religious leaders begin to oppose Jesus openly. Conflict is building.

The King's Secrets (Chapter 13). Jesus teaches in parables—stories with hidden meanings. The kingdom of heaven is like a mustard seed, like treasure hidden in a field, like a net catching fish. These stories reveal how God's kingdom works—and it's not what anyone expected.

The King Revealed (Chapters 14–17). The disciples slowly begin to understand who Jesus really is. Peter confesses, "You are the Messiah, the Son of the living God." Jesus is transfigured on a mountain, revealing his glory. But he also begins telling them something they don't want to hear: he must go to Jerusalem and die.

The King's Values (Chapters 18–20). Jesus teaches about life in the community of his followers. Forgive without limits. The last will be first. True greatness means becoming a servant. His kingdom turns the world's values upside down.

The King Confronts (Chapters 21–25). Jesus enters Jerusalem as a king, cleanses the temple, and clashes with the religious leaders. He tells parables of judgment and describes the end of the age. The tension is unbearable. Everyone knows something is about to break.

The King Conquers (Chapters 26–28). And here's where the story takes its shocking turn. The King is betrayed, arrested, tried, mocked, beaten, and crucified. It looks like total defeat. But on the third day, the tomb is empty. Jesus is alive. And in his final words, he claims all authority in heaven and earth and sends his followers to make disciples of every nation.

WHY THIS MATTERS

You might wonder why a book written two thousand years ago about events in a tiny country matters to your life today.

Here's why: the question Matthew asks is still the most important question anyone can answer. Who is Jesus?

Some people in Matthew's story said he was a prophet. Others said he was a fraud. The religious leaders said he was dangerous. The Roman governor said he was an inconvenience. His disciples said he was the Messiah, the Son of God.

Matthew wrote his book so you could make that decision for yourself. He lays out the evidence—the teachings, the miracles, the fulfilled prophecies, the death, the resurrection—and invites you to draw your own conclusion.

But here's the thing: Matthew doesn't think this is a neutral question. He doesn't present Jesus as one interesting option among many. He presents Jesus as the King—the one with all authority, the one who demands a response.

At the end of the book, Jesus tells his followers to teach new disciples "to obey everything I have commanded you." That's a big claim. It assumes that Jesus has the right to command. It assumes his words carry weight that lasts forever.

So as you read, pay attention. Watch what Jesus does. Listen to what he says. Notice how people respond to him—and notice how you respond.

Because Matthew isn't just telling you about something that happened long ago. He's introducing you to someone who's still alive, still reigning, and still calling people to follow him.

The wait is over. The King has come.

Turn the page.

1

THE KING ARRIVES

If you've ever watched a Marvel movie, you know the deal. Iron Man has his movie. Captain America has his. Thor, Black Panther, the Guardians of the Galaxy. Each film tells its own story. But the whole time, everything is connected. Characters cross paths. Events in one movie set up the next. Plot threads weave together across a dozen different films and a decade of storytelling, all building toward one massive event.

Now imagine opening the final movie and, before anything happens, the screen fills with a recap of *everything*. Not just the last film. All of them. Every hero, every turning point, every key moment compressed into a single sequence. That's what you're looking at when you open the book of Matthew. Because the very first thing Matthew gives you isn't a story. It isn't a miracle or a sermon or a manger scene.

It's a list of names.

Forty-two generations' worth of names, stretching from Abraham all the way to Jesus. And if that sounds boring, stick with me, because Matthew isn't wasting your time. He's doing something brilliant. He's showing you that every single story in the Old Testament has been building toward this one person. Abraham's faith, David's throne, the exile's heartbreak, the prophets' promises. All of it was headed somewhere. And now, finally, the destination has arrived.

The Gospel of Matthew is the story of Jesus. But before Matthew tells you what Jesus did, he wants you to understand who Jesus is. And who Jesus is can be summed up in two massive claims that Matthew makes in the very first verse of his book: Jesus is the son of David (the king Israel had been waiting for) and the son of Abraham (the one through whom God's ancient promises would come true).

Everything in these first two chapters flows from those two claims. The genealogy proves Jesus has the right to the throne. The birth story proves he was sent by God. The visit of the Magi shows that even outsiders recognized him. The rage of King Herod shows what happens when the true king threatens a fake one. And woven through all of it, like a drumbeat you can't miss, is Matthew's favorite phrase: *"This was to fulfill what the Lord had spoken through the prophet."*

Matthew uses that phrase five times in just these first two chapters. He wants you to know something beyond any doubt: Jesus didn't show up out of nowhere. He was planned. He was promised. He was the person every prophet had been pointing to for centuries.

Let's start at the beginning.

THE FAMILY TREE THAT TELLS A STORY

Most of us skip genealogies. We see a long list of hard-to-pronounce names and jump ahead to the good stuff. But Matthew's original readers wouldn't have done that. They were Jewish, and Jewish people cared deeply about family lineage. Your ancestry told people who you were, where you came from, and what you had a right to claim.

Matthew opens with a phrase that could be translated "the book of the origin of Jesus the Messiah." Then he gets right to it: Jesus is the son of David, the son of Abraham. Those two names aren't random. They're the two most important figures in Old Testament history when it comes to God's promises.

God promised Abraham that through his family all the nations of the earth would be blessed. That was way back in Genesis 12. God promised David that one of his descendants would sit on a throne that would last forever. That was in 2 Samuel 7. By calling Jesus the son of both men, Matthew is saying: this is the one. The blessing and the kingdom and the promise and the throne all come together in this baby.

Then Matthew organizes the genealogy into three neat sections of fourteen generations each: from Abraham to David, from David to the exile in Babylon, and from the exile to Jesus. That structure is deliberate. It turns Israel's messy, complicated history into a countdown. Abraham started the journey. David established the kingdom. The exile nearly destroyed everything. And now, after centuries of waiting, the clock has reached zero.

But there's something unexpected buried in this family tree. Matthew names four women, which was unusual for ancient genealogies. Even more unusual is *which* women he names. Not Sarah or Rebekah or Rachel, the famous wives of the patriarchs. Instead he names Tamar, Rahab, Ruth, and

Bathsheba (though he doesn't call her by name, only "the wife of Uriah"). If you know their stories, you know that each of these women had something scandalous, surprising, or unconventional about their role in Israel's history. And most of them were Gentiles, outsiders who got folded into God's plan.

Why does that matter? Because Matthew is already dropping hints about what the rest of his Gospel will reveal: God's plan was never just for one nation. The king born in this story didn't come for one group of people. He came for everyone. The outsiders were always part of the plan.

A PROBLEM, A DREAM, AND A NAME

After the genealogy, Matthew zooms in on the most important moment in the family tree: how the last name got added.

Mary was engaged to Joseph. In Jewish culture, engagement was a legally binding agreement, almost as serious as marriage itself. Before they came together as husband and wife, Mary was found to be pregnant.

Joseph knew the baby wasn't his. And being a righteous man who didn't want to publicly disgrace Mary, he decided to quietly break off the engagement. It was a merciful choice. In his culture, he could have made things much worse for her.

But then God stepped in. An angel appeared to Joseph in a dream and told him not to be afraid to take Mary as his wife. The child she carried was from the Holy Spirit. And the angel gave Joseph a specific instruction: name the boy Jesus, because he will save his people from their sins.

That name matters. "Jesus" means "the Lord saves." Every time someone said his name, they were speaking a tiny sermon. And notice what the angel said he would save people from. Not from the Romans. Not from political oppression. Not from poverty. From their *sins*. Right from the start, Matthew wants you to understand what kind of king Jesus would be. Not the military conqueror many in Israel were hoping for. A rescuer of a much deeper kind.

Then Matthew drops in his first fulfillment quotation. He points back to the prophet Isaiah, who hundreds of years earlier had said that a virgin would conceive and bear a son, and they would call him Immanuel, which means "God with us." Matthew isn't just checking a box. He's making a staggering claim: this child is God's presence arriving in person. The God who had been with Israel in a pillar of fire, in the tabernacle, in the temple, is now with his people in the most intimate way imaginable. As a baby. In a family. In the flesh.

Joseph woke up and did exactly what the angel told him. He took Mary as his wife. He named the baby Jesus. He didn't need to understand everything. He just obeyed.

THE WRONG KING AND THE RIGHT ONE

Chapter 2 opens with one of the most famous scenes in the Bible, but Matthew tells it in a way that might surprise you. He's less interested in the cute details of the Christmas story and more interested in a clash between two kings.

Jesus was born in Bethlehem during the reign of King Herod. Shortly after, a group of Magi arrived in Jerusalem from the east. These weren't kings, despite what the Christmas songs say. They were more likely scholars or royal advisors from Persia, men who studied the stars and ancient writings.

They showed up in the capital city with a question that sent shockwaves through the palace: "Where is the one who has been born king of the Jews? We saw his star when it rose and have come to worship him."

Think about what just happened. Foreigners from a distant country recognized something that the people of Jerusalem missed. They came looking for the true king. And when they asked their question, the reaction was telling. Herod was disturbed. And all Jerusalem with him.

Why was Herod so rattled? Because Herod was not the rightful king. He was an Idumean, not a descendant of David. He had been appointed by Rome, not anointed by God. He held his throne through political deals and brutal violence, not through any divine promise. History tells us that Herod was so paranoid about rivals that he executed members of his own family, including three of his own sons. The idea that a legitimate heir to David's throne had been born was a direct threat to everything Herod had built.

So Herod gathered the chief priests and scribes and asked them where the Messiah was supposed to be born. And here's something remarkable: they knew. They quoted the prophet Micah, who had written centuries earlier that out of Bethlehem would come a ruler who would shepherd God's people Israel. The religious leaders had the right information. They could point to the right verse. But they never went to Bethlehem to see for themselves.

The Magi did. They followed the star to the house where Jesus was. They fell down and worshiped him. They opened their treasures and presented gifts: gold, frankincense, and myrrh. Then, warned in a dream not to return to Herod, they went home by a different route.

Do you see the contrast Matthew is drawing? Gentile outsiders traveled hundreds of miles to find and worship the true king. The religious insiders who knew the prophecies didn't walk six miles down the road. And the ruling king responded not with worship but with murder.

INTO EGYPT AND BACK AGAIN

What happens next is dark. When Herod realized the Magi had left without reporting back to him, he was furious. He ordered his soldiers to kill every boy in Bethlehem who was two years old or younger. It was a horrific act, though sadly consistent with everything we know about Herod's character. Bethlehem was a small town, so the number of children was probably around twenty. That doesn't make it less tragic. It makes it personal. These were real families. Real grief.

But God had already moved to protect his son. Before the massacre, an angel appeared to Joseph in another dream: take the child and his mother, flee to Egypt, and stay there until I tell you it's safe.

Joseph obeyed. In the middle of the night, the family left for Egypt.

And here comes another fulfillment quotation, one that might seem puzzling at first. Matthew quotes the prophet Hosea: "Out of Egypt I called my son" (Hosea 1:1). In its original context, Hosea was talking about the nation of Israel, not the Messiah. God had called Israel, his "son," out of Egypt during the exodus.

So why does Matthew use it here? Because Matthew sees Jesus as the true Israel. Just as the nation went down into Egypt and was called back out, Jesus followed the same path. He was reliving Israel's story in his own life. The exodus of Israel was pointing forward to something bigger. And now that something bigger had arrived.

After Herod's death, an angel appeared to Joseph again: go back to the land of Israel, because those who were trying to kill the child are dead. The wording echoes what God told Moses when it was safe to return to Egypt after Pharaoh died. Matthew is drawing a line: Jesus is like a new Moses, a new deliverer, sent to lead God's people to freedom.

But when Joseph heard that Herod's son Archelaus was ruling in Judea, he was afraid to go there. Archelaus had inherited his father's cruelty without any of his competence. So, warned again in a dream, Joseph took the family to Nazareth in Galilee.

Matthew notes that even this fulfilled what the prophets had spoken: "He will be called a Nazarene." Nazareth was an obscure, unimpressive little village. Nobody expected anything important to come from there. But Matthew sees in that obscurity the fulfillment of a theme that runs through the prophets: the Messiah would come from humble, overlooked, even despised beginnings. The king of the universe grew up in a town that people made fun of.

WHAT THIS MEANS FOR US

First, God keeps his promises, even when it takes a very long time. The genealogy covers roughly two thousand years of history. That's two thousand years of waiting between Abraham's promise and Jesus' birth. Some of the people in that family tree never saw the promise fulfilled in their lifetime. But God never forgot. Every generation was a step closer to the goal. If you're waiting on God for something, Matthew 1 is a reminder that God's timeline and yours don't always match, but his faithfulness never fails.

Second, God works through imperfect people and unexpected circumstances. Look at the names in that genealogy. Liars, adulterers, idolaters, foreigners, and failures. God didn't wait for a perfect family line to send his son through. He worked through the mess. That means your mess isn't disqualifying. God has never needed perfect people to accomplish his purposes.

Third, pay attention to what kind of king Jesus is. From the very beginning, Jesus doesn't fit the expected mold. He's born in a small town, not a palace. He's visited by foreigners, not the religious establishment. He becomes a refugee before he can walk. His kingdom doesn't start with power and glory. It starts with vulnerability and obscurity. If you're looking for God to show up in flashy, impressive ways, you might miss him the same way Jerusalem missed the Magi's news.

Fourth, knowing the truth isn't the same as responding to it. The chief priests could quote Micah 5 from memory. They knew where the Messiah was to be born. But they didn't go. The Magi had far less information and traveled far farther. Knowledge without action is just trivia. What matters isn't just what you know about Jesus but what you do about it.

TALKING POINTS

1. **Matthew's genealogy includes people with messy, complicated, even scandalous stories.** Why do you think God chose to include those people in the family line of Jesus? What does that tell us about the kind of people God uses?

2. **Joseph didn't get an explanation for everything that was happening.** He got a dream and an instruction. Why do you think obedience sometimes has to come before understanding? Can you think of a time when you had to trust someone before you fully understood why?

3. **The Magi were outsiders who recognized Jesus, while the religious leaders in Jerusalem didn't bother to investigate.** What might cause people who are very familiar with the Bible to miss what God is actually doing? How can we guard against that?

4. **Herod saw Jesus as a threat to his power.** In what ways do people today resist the idea of Jesus being king over their lives? What are the "thrones" we don't want to give up?

5. **Matthew keeps pointing out that events in Jesus' life fulfilled Old Testament prophecy.** Why do you think that matters? What does it tell us about God's control over history?

The king has arrived. But he's not sitting on a throne. Not yet. He's a child in an obscure town, and almost nobody knows who he really is. That's about to change.

Turn the page.

2

TESTED BEFORE HE STARTS

In the movie *Mulan*, there's a stretch of the story that doesn't get talked about as much as the big battle scenes. It's the training. Mulan shows up at the army camp pretending to be a soldier, and before anyone will let her fight, she has to prove herself. She climbs the pole. She learns to fight. She gets knocked down, over and over, and gets back up. The other recruits doubt her. The captain almost sends her home.

But here's the thing: Mulan doesn't become who she is during the battle. She becomes who she is during the training. The battle just reveals what the training produced.

Matthew 3-4 is the training sequence in the story of Jesus. Before Jesus preaches a single sermon, before he heals a single person, before he calls a single disciple, Matthew shows us three things that had to happen first. A prophet had to announce him. God had to confirm him. And the enemy had to test him. Only after all three of those things does Jesus step into the public eye and begin the mission he came to accomplish.

These chapters might not have the drama of the Sermon on the Mount or the miracles that come later. But don't skip past them. Everything that follows depends on what happens here.

A VOICE IN THE WILDERNESS

Matthew jumps forward roughly thirty years between chapters 2 and 3. One moment Jesus is a toddler being carried to Egypt. The next, a wild-looking prophet is shouting in the desert. Matthew doesn't tell us anything about Jesus' childhood, his teenage years, or his twenties. He fast-forwards to the moment when everything starts moving.

That moment begins with John the Baptist.

John was a strange figure. He lived in the Judean wilderness, the rocky, desolate land between the hill country and the Dead Sea. He wore rough clothes made of camel's hair with a leather belt, a deliberate echo of the prophet Elijah from the Old Testament. His diet was locusts and wild honey, the kind of bare-minimum food that said, *I'm not here for comfort. I'm here with a message.*

And what a message it was. John's preaching can be boiled down to one explosive sentence: "Repent, for the kingdom of heaven is near." That word "repent" meant more than just feeling sorry. It meant turning your whole life around, changing direction completely, like someone who realizes they've been walking the wrong way on a trail and has to do a full one-eighty. And the reason for this urgency? The kingdom of heaven was at the door. God was about to act in history in a way he hadn't acted in centuries.

Matthew tells us that John fulfilled a prophecy from Isaiah, who had written about a voice calling in the wilderness to prepare the way of the Lord. In Isaiah's day, that image was about clearing and smoothing a road for a coming king. When royalty traveled in the ancient world, workers would go ahead and repair the roads. John was doing the same thing spiritually. He was preparing Israel's hearts for the arrival of their king.

And people responded. They came from Jerusalem, from all over Judea, from the regions around the Jordan River. They confessed their sins and were baptized in the river as a sign that they were serious about turning back to God.

But not everyone who showed up was sincere. When some of the Pharisees and Sadducees appeared (the two most powerful religious groups in Israel), John didn't roll out the welcome mat. He called them a "brood of vipers" and told them to prove their repentance with changed lives instead of hiding behind the fact that they were descendants of Abraham. Having the right family tree wasn't enough. God could make children of Abraham out of the rocks on the ground if he wanted to.

Then John said something that changed the temperature of the whole conversation. Someone was coming after him, he said, someone so much greater that John wasn't even worthy to carry his sandals. John baptized with water. This coming one would baptize with the Holy Spirit and with fire. John was the opening act. The headliner was about to take the stage.

THE DAY HEAVEN OPENED

Then Jesus showed up. He walked from Galilee to the Jordan River and asked John to baptize him. And John resisted. He knew who Jesus was. He said, in effect, "I'm the one who needs to be baptized by *you*. Why are you coming to me?"

It's a fair question. John's baptism was for repentance, for people who needed to confess their sins and turn back to God. Jesus didn't have sins to confess. So why did he want to be baptized?

Jesus' answer was brief and a little mysterious: "Let it be so now; it is proper for us to do this to fulfill all righteousness." In other words, this was something that needed to happen to complete God's plan. By being baptized, Jesus wasn't confessing sin. He was identifying with the people he came to save. He was stepping into their story, endorsing John's mission as genuinely from God, and publicly beginning his own.

John agreed. Jesus was baptized.

And then something extraordinary happened. As Jesus came up out of the water, the heavens opened. The Spirit of God descended on him like a dove. And a voice from heaven spoke: "This is my Son, whom I love; with him I am well pleased."

Stop and let that sink in. God the Father, God the Son, and God the Spirit, all present in the same moment. The Father speaks. The Son stands in the water. The Spirit descends. This isn't just a nice spiritual experience. It's a public coronation. God is announcing to the world who Jesus is.

And notice what the Father's words echo. "This is my Son" recalls Psalm 2, a royal psalm about the king God has chosen. "With him I am well pleased" echoes Isaiah 42, a passage about God's chosen servant who would bring justice to the nations. King and servant. Power and humility. Those two threads will run through the entire Gospel of Matthew, and they start right here, dripping wet at the Jordan River.

FORTY DAYS IN THE DESERT

You might expect that after such a powerful moment, Jesus would head straight into his ministry. Instead, the Spirit led him in the opposite direction. Into the wilderness. Alone. To be tempted by the devil.

For forty days and forty nights, Jesus fasted in the desert. That number isn't random. Israel wandered in the wilderness for forty years after leaving Egypt. Moses spent forty days on Mount Sinai receiving the law. In both cases, the wilderness was a place of testing. And now Jesus, the one Matthew has been presenting as the true Israel and the new Moses, faces his own wilderness test.

After forty days without food, Jesus was hungry. That's when the devil showed up with three temptations, each one designed to get Jesus to use his power in the wrong way.

The first temptation targeted the most basic human need: food. The devil said, "If you are the Son of God, tell these stones to become bread." It sounds reasonable. Jesus was starving. He had the power to do it. What's wrong with eating?

But the temptation wasn't really about bread. It was about whether Jesus would use his divine power to serve himself instead of trusting his Father. Jesus responded by quoting Deuteronomy: people don't live on bread alone but on every word that comes from God. Where Israel had grumbled about food in the wilderness and demanded that God provide, Jesus trusted his Father's timing and provision.

The second temptation was more dramatic. The devil took Jesus to the highest point of the temple in Jerusalem and said, "If you are the Son of God, throw yourself down. After all,

Scripture says God will send his angels to protect you." This time, the devil actually quoted the Bible. He pulled a verse from Psalm 91 about God's protection.

But he twisted it. There's a difference between trusting that God will protect you and deliberately throwing yourself into danger to force God to act. Jesus saw through it and quoted Deuteronomy again: you shall not put the Lord your God to the test. Where Israel had tested God at a place called Massah by demanding proof that God was with them, Jesus refused to turn trust into a stunt.

The third temptation dropped all pretense. The devil took Jesus to a high place, showed him all the kingdoms of the world and their splendor, and made a blunt offer: worship me, and I'll give you all of this. No cross. No suffering. No rejection. Just power, handed over immediately.

This was the real heart of it. Jesus had come to claim a kingdom, but God's plan required a path through suffering, rejection, and death. The devil was offering a shortcut. All it would cost was Jesus' soul.

Jesus' response was sharp and final: "Away from me, Satan! For it is written: 'Worship the Lord your God, and serve him only.'" Where Israel had repeatedly turned to false gods in the wilderness, Jesus refused to worship anyone but his Father. Three temptations. Three answers from Deuteronomy. Three victories where Israel had failed.

The devil left. And angels came and attended to Jesus.

Here's what you need to see: Jesus wasn't just resisting temptation for himself. He was succeeding where Israel had failed. He was proving himself to be the faithful Son that Israel never managed to be. Every answer he gave came from the same section of Deuteronomy that described Israel's failures in the wilderness. Matthew is telling us that Jesus is the true Israel, the one who finally gets it right.

LIGHT DAWNS IN GALILEE

After the temptation, Jesus heard that John the Baptist had been arrested. This signaled that it was time. Jesus left the wilderness and headed north to Galilee, settling not in his hometown of Nazareth but in a lakeside town called Capernaum.

And here comes Matthew's fulfillment drumbeat again. He quotes the prophet Isaiah, who had written about the land of Zebulun and Naphtali, a region near Galilee that Isaiah called "Galilee of the Gentiles." Isaiah said the people living in darkness had seen a great light. Matthew says Jesus is that light. By launching his public ministry in Galilee rather than Jerusalem, Jesus was fulfilling ancient prophecy and signaling that his mission was reaching beyond the expected boundaries.

Jesus began to preach, and his message was identical to John's: "Repent, for the kingdom of heaven is near." But now the message carried new weight. The one preaching it wasn't just the announcer. He was the king himself.

Then Jesus did something no ordinary rabbi would do. Walking along the Sea of Galilee, he called his first disciples. He found two brothers, Simon (called Peter) and Andrew, casting fishing nets into the lake. He said, "Follow me, and I will make you fishers of men." They left their nets immediately and followed him. A little farther on, he called two more brothers,

James and John, who were in a boat with their father Zebedee mending nets. They left the boat and their father and followed.

No applications to fill out. No interviews. No trial period. Jesus called, and they followed. The authority of his voice was enough.

Matthew closes this section with a summary that sets the stage for everything to come. Jesus went throughout Galilee teaching in synagogues, preaching the good news of the kingdom, and healing every disease and sickness among the people. Word spread across the entire region. People brought the sick, the demon-possessed, the paralyzed, those suffering severe pain. And Jesus healed them all. Large crowds from Galilee, from the Decapolis, from Jerusalem and Judea and the region beyond the Jordan began to follow him.

The king had been announced. He had been confirmed. He had been tested. Now his kingdom was breaking into the world, and nothing would be the same.

WHAT THIS MEANS FOR US

First, real change starts on the inside. John's message wasn't "clean up your behavior." It was "turn your whole life around." That's what repentance means. It's not just feeling bad about something you did. It's a complete change of direction that shows up in how you actually live. If someone says they've changed but nothing about their life is different, John would say the fruit doesn't match the claim.

Second, identity comes before activity. Before Jesus did anything in public, God declared who he was. "This is my Son, whom I love." Jesus didn't earn that identity by performing.

He received it from his Father. The same is true for you. Your value doesn't come from what you accomplish. It comes from who God says you are.

Third, temptation targets your God-given identity. Notice how the devil's first two temptations began: "If you are the Son of God…" He wasn't questioning whether Jesus was God's Son. He was trying to get Jesus to prove it in the wrong way. Temptation often works like that. It takes something true about you and twists it, pushing you to prove yourself, protect yourself, or promote yourself outside of God's plan.

Fourth, following Jesus costs something. Those fishermen didn't just add Jesus to their schedule. They left their nets, their boats, their father. Following Jesus rearranged their entire lives. It still does. That doesn't mean everyone has to quit their job. But it does mean Jesus gets the first word on how you spend your time, your energy, and your loyalty.

TALKING POINTS

1. **John the Baptist called people to repent, meaning to completely change direction.** What's the difference between being sorry about something and actually repenting? Why is one easier than the other?

2. **At his baptism, God declared that Jesus was his beloved Son before Jesus had done any public ministry.** What does it mean that God affirmed who Jesus was before Jesus "did" anything? How does that shape how you think about your own identity?

3. **Each of the devil's three temptations offered Jesus something that wasn't bad in itself (food, safety, power) but**

in the wrong way or at the wrong time. Can you think of examples in your own life where something good becomes a temptation because of the timing or the method?

4. **The first disciples dropped everything to follow Jesus.** What would it look like for someone your age to make following Jesus their top priority? What might that require giving up or rearranging?

5. **Matthew says Jesus was "a great light" dawning on people living in darkness.** What kinds of "darkness" do people your age experience? How does Jesus function as light in those situations?

The king has been announced, confirmed, tested, and now he's on the move. But what kind of kingdom is he building? What does life look like under his rule?

He's about to tell us. Turn the page.

3

THE KING'S MANIFESTO

In *Charlie and the Chocolate Factory*, five kids win golden tickets to tour the most amazing candy factory in the world. Most of them walk in thinking they already know how to win. Augustus is greedy and starts grabbing everything. Violet is competitive and has to be the best. Veruca is spoiled and demands whatever she wants. Mike thinks he's the smartest person in the room. One by one, each of them is knocked out of the tour by the very thing they thought made them great.

And then there's Charlie. He's the poorest kid in the group. He doesn't demand anything. He doesn't grab for more. He just listens, watches, and follows Wonka's lead. And at the end, Charlie is the one who inherits the entire factory. Not because he was the strongest or the smartest or the loudest. Because he was the kind of person Wonka was looking for all along.

Jesus does something similar in Matthew 5–7. These chapters contain what's traditionally called the Sermon on the Mount, the longest block of Jesus' teaching in any of the Gospels. Crowds have been gathering. Disciples have been called. And now, for the first time, the king sits down and explains how his kingdom actually works. But almost nothing he says lines up with what anyone expected. His teachings sound backwards, impractical, maybe even impossible.

They're not. They're the most revolutionary words ever spoken. And they turn everything you thought you knew about winning, losing, and what makes a person great completely on its head.

THE TEACHER TAKES HIS SEAT

Matthew opens this section with a quick but important scene. Jesus sees the crowds, goes up on a mountainside, and sits down. His disciples gather around him, and he begins to teach.

Every detail matters. The mountain echoes the great moments in Israel's history when God revealed himself, especially Mount Sinai, where Moses received the law. But Jesus isn't climbing the mountain to receive something from God. He's the one doing the teaching. He's not another Moses. He's greater than Moses.

And he sat down. In the Jewish world, that was the official teaching posture. When a rabbi stood, he might be reading Scripture or leading a discussion. But when he sat, it meant: "Pay attention. This is formal instruction." Jesus was speaking with full authority.

His main audience was his disciples, the people who had already committed to following him. But the crowds were listening too. Matthew tells us at the end of the sermon that the crowds were astonished at Jesus' teaching because he spoke as someone who had authority, not like their scribes. The scribes were the professional Bible teachers, and they always based their teaching on what earlier rabbis had said. Jesus quoted no one. He said, "You have heard that it was said … but I say to you." He taught as if he himself had the final word on what God wanted. Nobody had ever heard anything like it.

BLESSED ARE THE UNLIKELY

The sermon opens with a rapid-fire series of blessings that have come to be known as the Beatitudes. Each one names a group of people and declares them "blessed," which is better translated as "fortunate" or "to be congratulated."

But the people Jesus congratulates aren't the ones any first-century audience would have expected. He doesn't bless the powerful, the wealthy, the successful, or the popular. Instead, he blesses the poor in spirit, meaning those who recognize they have nothing to offer God on their own. He blesses those who mourn. The meek. Those who hunger and thirst for righteousness. The merciful. The pure in heart. The peacemakers. And those who are persecuted for doing what's right.

This is the upside-down kingdom in a nutshell. In the world's economy, power wins. In God's kingdom, humility wins. In the world's economy, you grab what you can. In God's kingdom, the meek inherit the earth. In the world's economy, people who get pushed around are losers. In God's kingdom, the persecuted are congratulated because they stand in the same line as the prophets.

The Beatitudes aren't a checklist of things you need to do to earn God's approval. They're a description of the kind of people who flourish when God is in charge. And notice that the first and last Beatitudes use the present tense: "theirs *is* the kingdom of heaven." The kingdom isn't just a future reward. It belongs to these people right now.

After the Beatitudes, Jesus tells his followers they are salt and light. Salt preserves and flavors. Light exposes and guides. A disciple who doesn't live like a disciple is like salt that's lost its taste or a lamp stuffed under a bucket. Useless. Jesus' followers are meant to affect the world around them, not blend into it.

GOING DEEPER THAN THE RULES

Now Jesus makes a statement that sets up everything that follows. He didn't come to abolish the Law or the Prophets. He came to fulfill them.

This was a big deal. The Torah (the first five books of the Bible) was the foundation of Jewish life. People might have wondered whether this new teacher was tossing out the old system. Jesus says the opposite. He's not throwing out the law. He's showing what it was always driving toward. He's taking it deeper, not lighter.

Then comes one of the most stunning sections in the entire Bible. Jesus takes six familiar teachings from the Old Testament and pushes each one far beyond what anyone had ever imagined.

The law says don't murder. Jesus says don't even harbor rage and contempt toward another person, because the destruction starts in the heart long before it reaches the hands. If you're about to worship God and remember that someone has something against you, stop what you're doing, go make it right, and then come back.

The law says don't commit adultery. Jesus says the problem begins with lust. It's not enough to avoid the act. God cares about what's happening inside you.

The law permitted divorce for various reasons, and the rabbis of Jesus' day argued about exactly which reasons qualified. Jesus cuts through the debate by pointing back to God's original design for marriage as a lifelong covenant. He treats it as something precious that shouldn't be discarded lightly.

The law allowed oaths to guarantee that someone was telling the truth. Jesus says his followers should be so consistently honest that oaths are unnecessary. Let your "yes" be "yes" and your "no" be "no."

The law set limits on revenge: an eye for an eye, a tooth for a tooth. That was actually a mercy law, preventing people from escalating payback beyond what was fair. But Jesus goes further. Don't retaliate at all. If someone insults you, don't trade insults back. If someone forces you to walk a mile carrying their gear, go two. Break the cycle of payback.

And the final, most radical teaching: the law said to love your neighbor. Popular interpretation added "and hate your enemy." Jesus says love your enemies and pray for those who persecute you. Why? Because God himself sends sun and rain on both the righteous and the unrighteous. If you only love people who love you back, you're no different from anyone else.

Jesus closes this section with a line that should stop every reader in their tracks: "Be perfect, as your heavenly Father is perfect." That word "perfect" is better understood as "whole" or "complete." Jesus isn't setting a standard you can check off. He's pointing to a direction: become the kind of person who reflects God's character. Grow toward wholeness. And the only way to get there is to let God do the work inside you.

THE HIDDEN LIFE

If chapter 5 is about how we treat other people, chapter 6 turns inward to how we relate to God. And the theme is simple: stop performing.

Jesus addresses three pillars of Jewish spiritual life: giving to the poor, prayer, and fasting. Each time, the pattern is the same. He describes the "hypocrites" (a word borrowed from the theater, literally meaning "actors") who turn their spiritual life into a public show. They give money with fanfare so everyone knows how generous they are. They pray loudly on street corners so people can admire their devotion. They make themselves look miserable when they fast so everyone knows how seriously they take God.

Jesus says do the opposite. Give in secret. Pray behind a closed door. Wash your face when you fast so nobody even knows. Because God sees what happens in secret, and his opinion is the only one that matters.

Tucked inside this section is the prayer that has become the most famous in history. Jesus offers it not as a script to recite mindlessly but as a pattern for how to pray. It begins with God's honor and God's agenda: let your name be treated as holy, let your kingdom come, let your will be done on earth as it is in heaven. Only after that does it turn to personal needs: give us bread for today, forgive us as we forgive others, and protect us from evil.

Did you catch the order? God's name. God's kingdom.

God's will. Then our needs. Most of us pray the other way around. We start with what we want and maybe get around to God's agenda at the end. Jesus says flip it.

And right at the center of this model prayer sits the request that captures the heartbeat of the entire sermon: "Your kingdom come, your will be done, on earth as it is in heaven." That's what everything in these three chapters is about. God's rule breaking into our world and changing the way things work.

THE REAL ENEMY: WORRY

The second half of chapter 6 tackles two closely related problems: the grip of money and the weight of anxiety.

Jesus says not to pile up treasures on earth, where they can be destroyed or stolen. Instead, invest in the things that matter to God's kingdom. Then he delivers a line that goes straight to the heart: where your treasure is, your heart will be also. You can figure out what someone truly worships by watching what they spend their time and money chasing.

He makes the stakes clear: no one can serve two masters. You'll either love one and resent the other, or hold to one and push the other aside. You cannot serve both God and money. Not "you shouldn't." You *can't.* They're pulling in opposite directions.

Then Jesus turns to worry, and his teaching here is some of the most comforting in all of Scripture. Look at the birds, he says. They don't plant crops or fill barns, and yet your heavenly Father feeds them. Look at the wildflowers. They don't work or sew their own clothes, and yet even King Solomon at the height of his glory wasn't dressed as beautifully as one of these.

If God cares for birds and flowers, which are here today and gone tomorrow, won't he care for you?

This isn't a call to be lazy or careless. It's a call to stop treating anxiety as your default setting. Worry adds nothing to your life. Instead, Jesus gives what might be the single best summary of the entire Sermon on the Mount: "Seek first the kingdom of God and his righteousness, and all these things will be given to you as well."

Put God's kingdom first. Everything else falls into line behind it.

CHOOSE YOUR FOUNDATION

The final chapter opens with a warning about judging others. Before you start critiquing the speck of sawdust in someone else's eye, deal with the plank in your own. Jesus isn't saying never evaluate anyone's behavior. He's saying start with yourself. Clean your own house before inspecting someone else's.

Jesus also encourages his followers to keep asking, seeking, and knocking in prayer, because God is a Father who loves giving good gifts to his children. Then he sums up the entire law in one line that we now call the Golden Rule: treat others the way you would want to be treated. That simple sentence, Jesus says, captures everything the Law and the Prophets were aiming at.

The sermon's conclusion hammers home one unavoidable point: listening to Jesus isn't enough. You have to act. He lays out three sharp contrasts that force a decision.

There are two gates. One is wide and comfortable, and it leads to destruction. The other is narrow and hard, and it leads to life. There are two kinds of trees. Good trees produce good fruit, and bad trees produce rotten fruit. You can identify people by the fruit their lives produce. And then there are two kinds of builders. One builds a house on solid rock. The other builds on sand. When the storm hits, the rock-built house stands, and the sand-built house collapses spectacularly.

Jesus saves his most sobering warning for the space between the trees and the builders. Some people will come to him on the day of judgment and say, "Lord, Lord, didn't we do incredible things in your name? Didn't we prophesy and cast out demons and perform miracles?" And Jesus will say, "I never knew you. Depart from me."

That's terrifying. And it's meant to be. The point isn't that spiritual gifts don't matter or that good deeds are worthless. The point is that none of that substitutes for actually doing the will of the Father. You can call Jesus "Lord" all day long and still be building on sand if your life doesn't match your words.

When Jesus finished, the crowds were astonished. Not just impressed. Astonished. Because he spoke with an authority that didn't come from quoting experts or citing traditions. It came from himself. He spoke as if he were the one who would judge the world.

According to Matthew, that's exactly who he is.

WHAT THIS MEANS FOR US

First, God's kingdom doesn't play by the world's rules. The Beatitudes announce that the people God favors aren't the ones the world applauds. If you've ever felt like you're too quiet, too sensitive, too ordinary, or too unpopular to matter, Jesus says you're exactly the kind of person his kingdom is built for.

Second, God wants your heart, not just your behavior. Every one of Jesus' deeper-than-the-law teachings makes the same move: he goes past the action to the attitude. You can follow every rule and still be rotten inside. Real change starts in the heart and works its way out.

Third, your spiritual life isn't a performance. Giving, praying, and fasting are good things. But the moment you do them to impress other people, they stop being about God and start being about you. The audience for your faith is an audience of one.

Fourth, you have to build, not just listen. It's possible to hear every sermon, read every chapter, know every Bible story, and still be building on sand. What separates the wise builder from the foolish one isn't how much they know. It's what they do with it.

TALKING POINTS

1. **The Beatitudes bless people who seem like underdogs: the humble, the grieving, the gentle, the persecuted.** Why do you think God's kingdom values these qualities instead of the ones our culture rewards?

2. **Jesus takes familiar rules like "don't murder" and pushes them deeper to include anger and contempt.** Is that fair? Why does Jesus care so much about what's happening on the inside?

3. **Jesus says to pray in secret, give in secret, and fast in secret.** In a world of social media where everything is public, what would it look like to practice your faith primarily for God's eyes?

4. **Jesus says you can't serve both God and money.** Do you think "money" could also stand for other things that compete for first place in your life? What are they?

5. **The sermon ends with a choice between two foundations.** What does it look like, practically, for someone your age to build their life on the rock of Jesus' teaching instead of on the sand of cultural expectations?

The king has revealed his vision. He's told us who is truly fortunate, how his people should live, and what foundation will hold when the storm comes. His words leave no room for spectators. They demand a response.

But can the king do more than talk? Can he actually bring the kingdom he described? Watch what happens next.

Turn the page.

4

THE KING'S PROOF

Have you ever watched a superhero movie where the hero gives a big speech about justice and saving the world, and then the very next scene throws them into a situation where they have to back it up? Think about *Spider-Man: Into the Spider-Verse*. Miles Morales can talk about being Spider-Man all he wants. But eventually, he has to jump off that building. He has to prove he can do what he says he can do.

That's exactly what happens in Matthew 8–9. In chapters 5–7, Jesus delivered the most stunning speech anyone had ever heard. He described life in the kingdom of God. He laid out a vision of the world as it should be, where the humble are blessed, enemies are loved, and God's will is done on earth as it is in heaven. Beautiful words. Revolutionary ideas.

But talk is cheap. Can this king actually do anything about the broken world he described?

Matthew answers that question with an explosion of action. In just two chapters, he records nine miracle stories containing ten actual miracles, and he makes clear that these are just samples from a much larger ministry. Jesus heals diseases, casts out demons, calms a deadly storm, forgives sins, and even raises a dead girl back to life. If chapters 5–7 showed Jesus' authority in his words, chapters 8–9 show his authority in his deeds.

The king isn't just talking. He's proving that the kingdom has arrived.

AUTHORITY OVER SICKNESS

The first three miracle stories aren't random. Matthew chose them carefully, and when you see who Jesus heals, the pattern becomes obvious. Each person represents a group that was pushed to the margins of Jewish society. Jesus crosses every barrier to reach them.

The leper. Leprosy in the ancient world wasn't necessarily the disease we call leprosy today. It was a blanket term for serious skin conditions that made a person ritually unclean. If you were labeled a leper, you were cut off from your community, your family, even your place of worship. You had to wear torn clothes, cover your face, and shout "Unclean!" to warn people to stay away. Some rabbis considered healing leprosy as difficult as raising someone from the dead.

This man breaks through all of that and kneels before Jesus. He says something remarkable: "Lord, if you are willing, you can make me clean." Notice what he gets right. He has total confidence in Jesus' power. He doesn't doubt for a second that Jesus *can* heal him. But he also has humility. He doesn't demand it. He leaves the decision in Jesus' hands.

And then Jesus does something that would have shocked everyone watching. He reached out and touched the man. Nobody touched lepers. Touching a leper made you ceremonially unclean under Jewish law. But instead of the uncleanness spreading from the leper to Jesus, Jesus' cleanness spreads to the leper. The disease vanishes instantly. Jesus doesn't just heal from a safe distance. He steps into the mess and makes it whole.

The centurion's servant. If the leper was an outcast because of his body, the centurion was an outsider because of his nationality. He was a Roman military officer, a Gentile, a representative of the empire that was occupying Israel. Many Jewish people would have despised him on sight.

But this centurion surprises everyone. He comes to Jesus begging for help, not for himself, but for his servant who is paralyzed and suffering terribly. When Jesus offers to come to his home, the centurion says he isn't worthy to have Jesus walk through his door. Instead, he asks Jesus to just say the word and his servant will be healed. His reasoning? As a military man, he understands authority. When he gives an order, soldiers obey, because behind his command stands the full power of Rome. He recognizes that behind Jesus' commands stands the full authority of God.

Jesus is *astonished*. That's a strong word. Matthew says Jesus hadn't found faith like this in all of Israel. Then Jesus makes a breathtaking announcement: many people will come from east and west (meaning from all nations, not just Israel) and sit down at the great feast in God's kingdom alongside Abraham, Isaac, and Jacob. Meanwhile, some who thought they had an automatic seat at the table will be left out.

This is a preview of the rest of the story. Faith, not ethnic heritage, is what connects a person to God's kingdom. And this Roman soldier, an outsider by every measure, understood Jesus' authority better than most of the people who had grown up with the Scriptures. The servant is healed at that very moment, without Jesus even going to the house.

Peter's mother-in-law. The third healing is the shortest but still significant. Jesus enters Peter's home, finds his mother-in-law sick with a fever, touches her hand, and heals her instantly. In a culture where women were often treated as second-class citizens, Jesus goes out of his way to care for her. And her response is immediate: she gets up and begins serving him.

Matthew then pulls back and gives us the big picture. That evening, crowds of sick and demon-possessed people were brought to Jesus, and he healed every one of them. Then Matthew quotes the prophet Isaiah: "He took up our infirmities and carried our diseases." This is from Isaiah 53, one of the most important prophecies about the coming Messiah. Matthew wants us to see that Jesus' healing ministry isn't random acts of kindness. It's the fulfillment of God's ancient promise. The suffering servant has arrived, and he's bearing the weight of human brokenness on his own shoulders.

AUTHORITY OVER EVERYTHING ELSE

The next section ratchets up the intensity. If the first three miracles showed Jesus' power over sickness, the next three show his power over nature, demons, and sin itself. But Matthew sandwiches them between two encounters about what it costs to follow Jesus.

Before the next miracle, two men approach Jesus about becoming followers. The first is a scribe who promises to follow

Jesus anywhere. Jesus tells him that foxes have holes and birds have nests, but the Son of Man has no place to lay his head. Translation: following me isn't glamorous. It might cost you your comfort.

The second man asks to first go bury his father (which probably means "let me wait until my father dies and I've settled family business"). Jesus replies with one of his most jarring statements: "Follow me, and let the dead bury their own dead." He isn't being cruel. He's saying that the call of the kingdom can't wait. Nothing gets to cut in line ahead of it.

These two encounters are placed right before some of Jesus' most dramatic miracles on purpose. Matthew is saying: yes, following Jesus is costly. But look at who you're following.

The storm. Jesus and his disciples get into a boat, and a violent storm erupts on the Sea of Galilee. The waves crash over the sides. The experienced fishermen among the disciples are terrified. And Jesus? He's asleep.

They wake him up, panicked. Jesus rebukes them for their lack of faith, then stands up and commands the wind and waves to stop. And they do. Instantly. Total calm.

The disciples are stunned. "What kind of man is this?" they ask. "Even the winds and the waves obey him!" That's exactly the right question, and it echoes through the rest of Matthew's Gospel. In the Old Testament, only God has authority over the sea and storms. The disciples are beginning to realize that whoever Jesus is, he's more than a teacher and more than a prophet.

The demons. On the other side of the lake, Jesus encounters two men controlled by demons. They live in burial caves, too violent for anyone to pass through the area. The demons recognize Jesus immediately and cry out in fear, calling him the Son of God. They know who he is, and they know their time is limited.

Jesus casts the demons out, and they enter a herd of pigs that rushes down a cliff into the lake. When the nearby townspeople hear what happened, they come out to meet Jesus, but instead of thanking him, they beg him to leave. The pigs were worth money. A man who could do this kind of thing was terrifying. They preferred their familiar problems to the uncomfortable power of the King.

It's a sobering detail. Some people see what Jesus can do and worship. Others see the same thing and walk away because the cost feels too high.

The paralytic. Back in Capernaum, some men bring a paralyzed friend to Jesus on a mat. When Jesus sees their faith, he says something nobody expected: "Take heart, son; your sins are forgiven."

Wait. They brought the man for healing. Why is Jesus talking about sin?

The religious leaders in the room are furious. In their minds, only God can forgive sins. By claiming to do it, Jesus is committing blasphemy, the worst possible offense.

But Jesus knows what they're thinking. So he asks them a question: which is easier to say, "Your sins are forgiven," or "Get up and walk"? Both are impossible for a human being. But to prove that he actually has authority to forgive sins (which you can't see), he heals the paralysis (which you can see). He tells the man to stand up, pick up his mat, and go home. And the man does.

This is a turning point. Jesus isn't just a healer. He has the authority to do something only God can do: forgive sins. The crowd is amazed. The religious leaders are furious. The lines are starting to be drawn.

THE KINGDOM CHANGES EVERYTHING

After healing the paralytic, Jesus does something else that offends the religious establishment. He calls a tax collector named Matthew to follow him, and then he eats dinner at Matthew's house with a crowd of tax collectors and sinners.

Tax collectors in Israel were Jewish men who worked for Rome, collecting money from their own people to fund the occupying empire. They were despised as traitors and were considered ceremonially unclean. Respectable religious teachers didn't associate with them. They certainly didn't eat with them. Sharing a meal in the ancient world was an act of acceptance and friendship.

When the Pharisees see this, they're scandalized. Why does your teacher eat with tax collectors and sinners? Jesus' answer cuts to the heart of his entire mission: "It is not the healthy who need a doctor, but the sick. I have not come to call the righteous, but sinners."

Then some of John the Baptist's followers ask why Jesus' disciples don't fast the way they and the Pharisees do. Jesus responds with two quick illustrations. You don't sew a new piece of cloth onto an old garment, because the patch will shrink and tear the old fabric apart. And you don't pour new wine into old wineskins, because the fermenting wine will burst the brittle skins. The point? What God is doing through Jesus can't be squeezed into the old categories. The kingdom requires new ways of thinking, new practices, and new priorities. Something brand new is happening, and it demands a fresh response.

FAITH, SIGHT, AND GROWING OPPOSITION

The final section of chapters 8–9 gives us three more miracles, and now the responses to Jesus start to sharply divide.

A dead girl and a desperate woman. A synagogue leader comes to Jesus in agony. His daughter has just died. He believes that if Jesus will just come and touch her, she'll live. That's extraordinary faith from a man who's part of the religious establishment.

On the way to the ruler's house, a woman who has been bleeding for twelve years sneaks up behind Jesus and touches the edge of his cloak. Her condition would have made her socially isolated for over a decade. She's desperate. She believes that just touching his clothes will be enough.

Jesus turns, sees her, and says, "Take heart, daughter; your faith has made you well." She is healed instantly.

Then Jesus arrives at the ruler's house, sends out the mourners, takes the dead girl by the hand, and raises her to life. Notice: he touches a dead body, which would make a person ceremonially unclean. But like the leper, death's uncleanness can't contaminate Jesus. Instead, his life overpowers death itself.

Two blind men and a mute man. Two blind men follow Jesus, calling him "Son of David," a title that identifies him as the promised Messiah. Jesus asks if they believe he can heal them. They say yes. He touches their eyes and their sight is restored.

Then a man who can't speak is brought to Jesus. He's controlled by a demon. Jesus drives the demon out and the man speaks.

The crowd's reaction? "Nothing like this has ever been seen in Israel." The Pharisees' reaction? "He drives out demons by the prince of demons." Same evidence. Opposite conclusions. This split will only get wider as Matthew's story continues.

THE HARVEST AND THE CALL

Matthew closes this section with a summary that echoes 4:23 almost word for word. Jesus traveled through all the towns and villages, teaching in their synagogues, preaching the good news of the kingdom, and healing every disease and sickness. Everything that happened in chapters 5–9 is just a sample of a much larger ministry.

But then Matthew adds something new. When Jesus saw the crowds, he had compassion on them because they were harassed and helpless, like sheep without a shepherd. The religious leaders who were supposed to guide them had failed. So Jesus tells his disciples to pray and ask the Lord to send out workers into the harvest.

That prayer is about to be answered. In the next chapter, Jesus sends out his twelve disciples to do the very things he's been doing: preach the kingdom and heal the sick. The mission isn't just his. It's becoming theirs. And eventually, it will become ours.

WHAT THIS MEANS FOR US

First, Jesus doesn't just announce the kingdom. He demonstrates it. Every healing, every exorcism, every calmed storm is proof that God's power is breaking into the world through Jesus. The kingdom isn't just an idea. It's an invasion.

Second, Jesus crosses every barrier to reach people. Lepers, Gentiles, women, tax collectors, the demon-possessed, the ritually unclean. Nobody is too far gone, too far outside, or too contaminated for Jesus to touch. If you've ever felt like you don't belong, these chapters are written for you.

Third, Jesus' authority goes beyond physical healing. The paralytic story makes this unmistakable. Healing bodies is impressive. Forgiving sins is divine. Jesus claims to do both, and he backs it up.

Fourth, seeing isn't always believing. The crowds and the Pharisees watched the same miracles. The crowds were amazed. The Pharisees accused Jesus of working for the devil. Evidence alone doesn't produce faith. Something has to happen in the heart.

TALKING POINTS

1. **Jesus touched a leper, ate with tax collectors, and raised a dead girl by taking her hand.** Why do you think Jesus kept crossing boundaries that other religious leaders avoided?

2. **The centurion understood Jesus' authority better than anyone in Israel, even though he was a Gentile outsider.** What does that tell us about what real faith looks like?

3. **Jesus calmed a storm with a word. The disciples asked, "What kind of man is this?"** How would you answer that question based on what you've read so far in Matthew?

4. **The Pharisees watched Jesus heal a man and accused him of using the devil's power.** Why do you think some

people reject what's right in front of them? Have you ever seen that happen?

5. Jesus told his disciples to pray for more workers for the harvest. What does it mean for someone your age to be part of that harvest?

The king has spoken, and now he's acted. His words carry authority. His touch brings healing. His presence changes everything it contacts. But not everyone is celebrating. The religious leaders are getting suspicious, and the opposition is growing.

What happens when the king sends his followers to do the same things he's been doing? That's next.

Turn the page.

5

SENT OUT AND SECOND THOUGHTS

In *The Hunger Games*, there's a moment when Katniss Everdeen stops being a survivor and becomes something else. The leaders of the rebellion hand her a weapon, put her in front of a camera, and tell her she's no longer just a girl from District 12. She's the Mockingjay. She's been given a mission: carry the message, inspire the districts, and expect the Capitol to fight back with everything it has.

It doesn't go the way anyone planned. Some people rally to the cause. Others turn hostile. And even the people who believe in what she's doing start having doubts about whether it's actually working.

In Matthew 10–11, Jesus has been preaching the kingdom and demonstrating it with miracle after miracle. Now he does something that changes the game: he hands his mission to his disciples. He gives them his authority, sends them out with his message, and warns them that the world is going to push back hard. Then, in chapter 11, even his greatest supporter starts having second thoughts about whether Jesus is really who he claimed to be.

These two chapters are about what it means to carry the king's mission into a world that doesn't always want to hear it.

THE TWELVE GET THEIR ORDERS

At the end of chapter 9, Jesus looked at the crowds and felt deep compassion for them. They were harassed and helpless, like sheep without a shepherd. The religious leaders who were supposed to guide them had failed. So Jesus told his disciples to pray for God to send workers into the harvest. Now the answer to that prayer arrives, and it's them.

Jesus calls his twelve disciples together and gives them authority to drive out evil spirits and heal every disease and sickness. This is the same authority Jesus himself has been exercising throughout chapters 8–9. He isn't just asking them to talk about the kingdom. He's empowering them to demonstrate it, the same way he did.

Matthew gives us the names of the twelve. It's a fascinating group. You've got fishermen like Peter, Andrew, James, and John. You've got Matthew the tax collector, a man who used to work for Rome. You've got Simon the Zealot, a man associated with the movement that wanted to overthrow Rome by force. A tax collector and a revolutionary in the same band of followers. Only Jesus could hold that group together.

Then Jesus gives them their marching orders. For now, they're to go only to the lost sheep of Israel, not to Gentile or Samaritan towns. This isn't because Gentiles don't matter. Jesus has already healed a Roman centurion's servant and predicted that people from every nation would sit at God's table. But the mission starts with Israel. The disciples aren't ready yet to cross major cultural boundaries, and God's ancient promises to Israel come first in the storyline. Later, after the resurrection, Jesus will send them to all nations.

Their message is identical to Jesus' own: "The kingdom of heaven is near." And their ministry mirrors his exactly: heal the sick, raise the dead, cleanse those with skin diseases, cast out demons. They received this power as a gift, so they should give it as a gift. No charging for miracles.

Jesus also tells them to travel light. No extra money, no extra clothes, no bag. When they enter a town, they should find a worthy household and stay there. If people welcome them, wonderful. If not, they're to shake the dust off their feet and move on. That gesture had serious meaning. Jewish people would shake the dust of Gentile lands off their feet when they returned to Israel. By doing this in a Jewish town, the disciples were saying, "You've rejected God's message. That puts you on the outside."

GET READY FOR TROUBLE

Now the tone shifts dramatically. Jesus has told them what to do. Now he tells them what will happen to them when they do it. "I am sending you out like sheep among wolves," he says. "So be as shrewd as snakes and as innocent as doves."

That's not a comforting image. He's telling them straight up: this is dangerous. People will hand you over to local councils. You'll be flogged in synagogues. You'll be dragged before governors and kings because of me. Brothers will betray brothers. Parents will turn against children. You will be hated by everyone because of my name.

If this sounds like it goes beyond what twelve guys experienced on a short preaching trip through Galilee, that's because it does. Matthew includes these warnings because they applied not only to the original twelve but to every generation of Jesus' followers. The mission Jesus launched didn't end when those twelve came back. It continued into the early church, where Christians faced exactly the kind of persecution Jesus described. And it continues today.

But woven into the warnings are promises. When you're arrested, don't worry about what to say. The Spirit of your Father will speak through you. Don't be afraid of those who can kill the body but can't touch the soul. God watches over every sparrow that falls, and you are worth far more than many sparrows. Even the hairs on your head are numbered. Your Father knows you completely, and he hasn't lost track of you.

Jesus tells his followers that whoever acknowledges him before others, he will acknowledge before his Father in heaven. And whoever denies him before others, he will deny before the Father. The stakes are real. This isn't a game.

THE SWORD, NOT PEACE

Then Jesus says something that shocks most people the first time they read it: "Do not suppose that I have come to bring peace to the earth. I did not come to bring peace, but a sword."

Wait. Isn't Jesus the Prince of Peace? Didn't he just bless the peacemakers in the Sermon on the Mount?

He did. But he's making a different point here. He's not saying he wants conflict. He's saying that following him will *cause* conflict, because not everyone will accept the message.

Families will split over it. A person's enemies may be the people in their own household. Choosing to follow Jesus will sometimes mean standing alone when the people closest to you don't understand.

Jesus doesn't soften this. He says that anyone who loves their father or mother more than him isn't worthy of him. Anyone who loves their son or daughter more than him isn't worthy of him. Whoever doesn't take up their cross and follow him isn't worthy of him.

That cross language is sharper than we sometimes realize. In the Roman world, the cross was an instrument of execution reserved for criminals and rebels. Jesus' audience knew exactly what carrying a cross meant: you were on your way to die. Following the king means being willing to lose everything for his sake.

And then comes one of Jesus' great paradoxes: "Whoever finds their life will lose it, and whoever loses their life for my sake will find it."

YOU REPRESENT THE KING

The chapter ends on a warmer note. Jesus tells his disciples that whoever receives them receives him, and whoever receives him receives the Father who sent him. This is the language of authorized agents. In the ancient world, how you treated someone's official representative was the same as how you treated the person who sent them. The disciples aren't just random preachers. They carry the authority of the King himself.

And it doesn't take a grand gesture to participate in the mission. Even giving a cup of cold water to one of these "little ones" because they're a follower of Jesus will not go unrewarded. God notices the smallest acts of kindness done in Jesus' name.

JOHN THE BAPTIST HAS SECOND THOUGHTS

Chapter 11 opens with a shift. Jesus goes on teaching and preaching in Galilee, but the focus moves to John the Baptist, who is now sitting in prison. Herod Antipas had arrested him (Matthew will explain the full story later in chapter 14), and John is hearing reports of what Jesus has been doing.

And here's the surprising part: John sends his own disciples to ask Jesus a question. "Are you the one who was to come, or should we expect someone else?"

Think about that for a moment. This is the same John who baptized Jesus in the Jordan River. The same John who saw the heavens open and the Spirit descend. The same John who declared that he wasn't even worthy to untie Jesus' sandals. And now he's asking, "Are you really the guy?"

Why? Most likely because things weren't going the way John expected. John had preached that the Messiah would bring fiery judgment, separating the wheat from the chaff. Instead, Jesus was healing the sick, eating with sinners, and preaching good news to the poor. And John was still in prison. If the Messiah had come, why wasn't the world changing the way John thought it would?

Jesus doesn't scold John for doubting. Instead, he sends a message back: "Tell John what you hear and see. The blind receive sight. The lame walk. Those with skin diseases are cleansed. The deaf hear. The dead are raised. And the good news is preached to the poor." Every item on that list echoes the promises of Isaiah about what would happen when God's kingdom arrived. Jesus is saying: the kingdom is here. It just doesn't look the way you expected.

Then he adds a gentle but pointed line: "Blessed is anyone who does not stumble on account of me." In other words: don't let your expectations about what the Messiah should do keep you from recognizing what the Messiah is actually doing.

After John's disciples leave, Jesus turns to the crowd and speaks about John with incredible respect. John was no weakling blown around by the wind. He was no pampered celebrity in fine clothes. He was a prophet, and more than a prophet. He was the messenger sent to prepare the way, the one the Old Testament itself predicted. Jesus says that among everyone ever born, no one has been greater than John the Baptist.

But then Jesus adds something unexpected: yet the least person in the kingdom of heaven is greater than John. Not because they're more devoted or more courageous, but because they live on this side of the cross and resurrection. They have access to a fuller picture of what God is doing than even John could see from his prison cell.

A GENERATION THAT WON'T BE SATISFIED

Jesus then turns his attention to the people of his generation, and his words are sharp. He compares them to children sitting in the marketplace, complaining that nobody will play the game they want to play. John came fasting and living in the wilderness, and people said he had a demon. Jesus came eating and drinking and attending parties, and people called him a glutton and a friend of sinners. The generation rejected both approaches.

They didn't want a prophet of mourning, and they didn't want a prophet of celebration. They just didn't want to listen.

Then Jesus pronounces judgment on the cities where most of his miracles had been performed: Chorazin, Bethsaida, and Capernaum. These towns had front-row seats to the kingdom of God, and they yawned. Jesus says that the ancient pagan cities of Tyre and Sidon would have repented long ago if they had seen what these Jewish cities saw. Even Sodom would have survived.

The principle is sobering: the more you've seen and heard of the truth, the more responsible you are for what you do with it. Privilege isn't a free pass. It's a higher standard.

COME TO ME

The chapter ends with one of the most beautiful passages in the entire Gospel. After pronouncing judgment on the stubborn and self-satisfied, Jesus turns and praises his Father for hiding the truth from the wise and learned and revealing it to little children. The religious experts missed it. The humble and broken received it.

Then Jesus makes a staggering claim about his own identity. All things have been committed to him by the Father. No one knows the Son except the Father, and no one knows the Father except the Son and those to whom the Son chooses to reveal him.

Read that again. Jesus is claiming a relationship with God that nobody else has. He's not just a teacher pointing people toward God. He's the only way to know God. This is one of the clearest statements in Matthew about who Jesus really is.

And then comes the invitation that has drawn weary people to Jesus for two thousand years: "Come to me, all you who are weary and burdened, and I will give you rest. Take my yoke upon you and learn from me, for I am gentle and humble in heart, and you will find rest for your souls. For my yoke is easy and my burden is light."

A yoke was the wooden frame placed on oxen to guide them as they plowed. Jewish teachers talked about the "yoke of the law," meaning the obligation to obey God's commands. But the religious leaders of Jesus' day had loaded that yoke with endless rules and traditions until it crushed people. Jesus offers a different yoke. Not lighter because he demands less (his standards are actually higher than the Pharisees'), but lighter because he walks beside you and carries the weight with you. The religious leaders piled burdens on people and didn't lift a finger to help. Jesus shares the load.

WHAT THIS MEANS FOR US

First, the mission isn't just for professionals. Jesus sent ordinary, unpolished people to do extraordinary work. If you think you're not qualified to represent the king, you're in good company. None of the twelve were.

Second, following Jesus will cost you something. He never pretended otherwise. The promise isn't comfort and popularity. The promise is that the God who counts every sparrow and numbers every hair on your head will never lose sight of you, no matter what you face.

Third, it's okay to have honest questions. John the Baptist doubted from a prison cell, and Jesus didn't reject him for it.

He answered the question. If your faith feels shaky sometimes, bring your doubts to Jesus. He can handle them.

Fourth, Jesus offers rest for the weary, not the self-impressed. The people who find Jesus are not the ones who think they've got everything figured out. They're the ones who know they're tired, burdened, and in over their heads. Those are exactly the people Jesus is calling.

TALKING POINTS

1. **Jesus sent out ordinary people with extraordinary authority.** What does it tell you about God's kingdom that he chose fishermen and tax collectors instead of religious professionals?

2. **Jesus warned his followers they would be hated and persecuted.** How does that change the way you think about what it means to follow Jesus? Is that warning still relevant today?

3. **John the Baptist had doubts about Jesus even after all he had seen and heard.** Why do you think doubt is a normal part of faith? How did Jesus respond to John's doubt?

4. **Jesus said the people of Chorazin and Bethsaida would be judged more harshly because they had seen more.** What does that mean for people today who have access to Bibles, churches, and Christian teaching?

5. **Jesus invites the weary and burdened to come to him for rest.** What are the "heavy burdens" someone your age might carry? What would it look like to bring those to Jesus?

The mission has been launched. The disciples have their orders. But not everyone is cheering. Doubts are creeping in, cities are refusing to repent, and the religious leaders are growing more hostile by the day. The tension is about to explode. And when it does, Jesus will have to explain why his kingdom looks so different from what everyone expected.

Turn the page.

6

BATTLE LINES AND SECRET STORIES

Have you ever had two friends who just could not get along? No matter what one of them said or did, the other found a reason to be upset about it. If the first friend was quiet, they got called stuck-up. If they were outgoing, they got called annoying. After a while, you realized the problem wasn't anything specific. The second friend had just decided not to like the first one, and everything after that was an excuse.

That's what happens in Matthew 12. The tension between Jesus and the religious leaders that has been building for several chapters finally boils over. The Pharisees have made up their minds about Jesus. It doesn't matter what he does. If he heals on the wrong day, he's a lawbreaker. If he casts out a demon, he's working for the devil. They've decided he's the enemy, and they start looking for ways to destroy him.

And then, in chapter 13, something shifts. Jesus starts teaching in a completely different way. Instead of straightforward sermons, he tells stories called parables. Strange, vivid stories about farmers and weeds and hidden treasure and fishing nets. Stories that made some people lean in closer and others walk away confused. And that was exactly the point.

These two chapters mark a turning point in Matthew's Gospel. The battle lines are drawn, and Jesus responds by revealing the kingdom's secrets to those who are willing to listen.

TWO FIGHTS ABOUT THE SABBATH

The trouble starts on a Saturday, the Jewish Sabbath. Jesus and his disciples are walking through some grain fields, and the disciples are hungry. They pluck a few heads of wheat and eat them. This was perfectly legal. The Old Testament allowed travelers to eat from someone else's field as they passed through. But the Pharisees pounce. In their view, plucking grain counted as "reaping," and reaping was one of thirty-nine activities their traditions specifically banned on the Sabbath.

Jesus doesn't back down. He fires back with three arguments, each one sharper than the last. First, he brings up King David. When David and his men were on the run from Saul and starving, they went to the tabernacle and ate the sacred bread that was reserved for priests. God didn't condemn David for it. Human need mattered more than ritual restrictions.

Second, Jesus points out that the priests themselves "break" the Sabbath every week by working in the temple, offering sacrifices and performing their duties. The law itself made room for exceptions.

Third, and most importantly, Jesus drops a bombshell: "Something greater than the temple is here." He's talking about himself. If temple service could override the Sabbath, how much more could the presence of the one the temple pointed to? Then he quotes the prophet Hosea: "I desire mercy, not sacrifice." God has always cared more about compassion than about ritual performance. And Jesus finishes with a claim that must have made the Pharisees' blood boil: "The Son of Man is Lord of the Sabbath."

"Lord of the Sabbath." That means Jesus has authority over the Sabbath itself. He gets to say what it means and how it works. That's not the claim of a rabbi with a different opinion. That's the claim of someone who stands above the law because he's the one the law was always pointing to.

The second confrontation happens immediately. Jesus enters a synagogue where a man has a paralyzed hand. The Pharisees are watching, hoping Jesus will heal the man so they can accuse him of working on the Sabbath.

Jesus asks them a simple question: if one of your sheep fell into a pit on the Sabbath, wouldn't you pull it out? Of course you would. And isn't a person worth more than a sheep? So it must be lawful to do good on the Sabbath.

Then he tells the man to stretch out his hand. The man obeys, and the hand is completely healed. Jesus didn't mix any medicine. He didn't perform any physical labor. He just spoke, and God healed.

The Pharisees' response? They leave and begin plotting how to kill him. Think about how upside-down that is. Jesus healed a man's hand, and they responded by planning a murder. Their devotion to their rules had become so rigid that they couldn't see God at work right in front of them.

THE SERVANT WHO WON'T FIGHT BACK

After this, Jesus withdraws. He's not running from a fight. His time hasn't come yet, and he has more work to do before the cross. Matthew tells us that Jesus continued healing everyone who came to him but warned people not to spread the word about who he was.

Then Matthew does something he loves to do: he quotes the Old Testament. This time it's a long passage from Isaiah 42, one of the "servant songs" that describe God's chosen servant. The prophecy describes someone gentle and quiet, someone who won't argue in the streets or crush the weak. A bruised reed he won't break. A flickering candle he won't blow out. And yet this servant will ultimately bring justice to the nations.

This is Matthew's way of saying: don't misread Jesus' withdrawal as weakness. He's not the kind of Messiah who comes with a sword and an army. He's the suffering servant, and his gentleness is deliberate. His victory will come, but not the way anyone expected.

THE UNFORGIVABLE ACCUSATION

The conflict escalates fast. Jesus heals a man who is blind and mute because of a demon. The crowds are stunned and begin asking the question Matthew has been building toward for chapters: "Could this be the Son of David?" In other words, is this the Messiah?

The Pharisees hear the whispers and shut them down with the most serious accusation they can make: "It is only by Beelzebul, the prince of demons, that this fellow drives out demons." They can't deny the miracle happened. So instead, they claim Jesus gets his power from Satan.

Jesus dismantles their argument piece by piece. First, why would Satan cast out his own forces? A kingdom divided against itself can't stand. Second, other Jewish leaders also cast out demons. Are they working for Satan too? Third, and most critically, if Jesus is driving out demons by the Spirit of God, then the kingdom of God has arrived. The demons aren't being quietly reassigned. They're being forcibly expelled because someone stronger than Satan has shown up and is taking back what the enemy stole.

Then Jesus issues one of the most sobering warnings in the entire Gospel. Every sin and blasphemy can be forgiven, he says, but blasphemy against the Holy Spirit will not be forgiven. This isn't about a single careless word. It's about what the Pharisees were doing: watching the Holy Spirit work through Jesus and deliberately, persistently calling it the work of the devil. They had seen the evidence. They understood what was happening. And they chose to reject it anyway, attributing God's work to Satan. That kind of hardness eventually makes repentance impossible, not because God won't forgive, but because the heart becomes too calloused to ask.

A WICKED GENERATION AND JESUS' TRUE FAMILY

Some Pharisees and teachers of the law then ask Jesus for a miraculous sign. After everything they've just seen, they want more proof. Jesus calls them a wicked and adulterous generation. The only sign they'll get is the sign of the prophet Jonah: just as Jonah spent three days in the belly of the great fish, the Son of Man will spend three days in the heart of the earth. This is one of Jesus' earliest hints about his coming death and resurrection.

Then he makes a stinging comparison. The people of Nineveh repented when Jonah preached to them, and all Jonah did was deliver a message. The Queen of Sheba traveled a great distance to hear Solomon's wisdom. Yet someone greater than Jonah and greater than Solomon is standing right here, and this generation still refuses to listen. People with far less evidence responded better than the people with the most.

The chapter ends with a personal scene. Jesus' own mother and brothers show up wanting to speak with him. Instead of rushing out to meet them, Jesus gestures toward his disciples and says that whoever does the will of his Father in heaven is his brother, sister, and mother. He's not rejecting his family. He's redefining what family means in the kingdom. Spiritual kinship through obedience to God runs deeper than blood.

WHY JESUS STARTED TELLING STORIES

Chapter 13 marks a major shift in how Jesus teaches. He leaves the house, sits down by the lake, and starts telling parables to the crowds. A parable is a short story drawn from everyday life that carries a deeper meaning. Jewish teachers used parables all the time. But Jesus uses them in a unique way: they simultaneously reveal truth to his followers and conceal it from those who have already decided not to listen.

When the disciples ask him why he's teaching this way, Jesus explains that the secrets of the kingdom have been given to them but not to the crowds. Then he quotes Isaiah: people will hear but not understand, see but not perceive. Their hearts have become hard.

This sounds harsh, but it's not arbitrary. The people who pressed close to Jesus, who followed him and asked questions and stayed after the crowds went home, received the full explanation. The parables rewarded curiosity and punished indifference. If you wanted to understand, you could. But if you'd already closed your ears, the stories would remain riddles.

THE PARABLE OF THE SOILS

The first and longest parable is about a farmer scattering seed. Some falls on a hard path and birds eat it. Some falls on rocky ground where it sprouts quickly but dies because the roots can't go deep. Some falls among thorns that choke it out. And some falls on good soil and produces an enormous harvest.

Jesus explains the parable privately to his disciples. The seed is the message of the kingdom. The different soils represent different kinds of responses.

The path represents someone who hears the message but doesn't understand it, and the devil snatches it away. The rocky ground is someone who receives it with excitement but has no depth. When trouble or persecution comes because of the message, they bail. The thorny ground is someone who hears the word, but the worries of life and the attraction of wealth slowly strangle it out. And the good soil? That's the person who hears, understands, and produces a life that shows it.

Notice: three out of four soils fail. Jesus isn't naïvely optimistic about how many people will respond to the kingdom. He knows most won't. But the one soil that works produces a harvest so abundant that it more than makes up for the rest.

WEEDS, SEEDS, AND HIDDEN THINGS

Jesus then tells a string of parables that all circle around the same idea: the kingdom of God is present right now, but it's hidden, and it won't be fully revealed until the end.

The parable of the weeds is the most developed. A farmer plants good seed, but an enemy sneaks in at night and plants weeds among the wheat. As both grow together, the workers want to pull up the weeds. But the farmer says no. Wait until harvest. Then we'll separate them. Pulling the weeds now would risk destroying the wheat.

Later, Jesus explains this parable to the disciples. The farmer is the Son of Man. The field is the world. The good seed represents the people of the kingdom, and the weeds are the people of the evil one. The enemy is the devil. The harvest is the end of the age, when the angels will finally sort everything out.

The point? God's kingdom and the world's evil exist side by side right now. That's frustrating. We want God to fix everything immediately. But God is patient. He lets things grow together because he values the wheat too much to risk uprooting it along with the weeds. The separation is coming, but it comes on God's schedule, not ours.

The parables of the mustard seed and the yeast make a similar point from a different angle. The mustard seed is tiny, almost invisible, but it grows into a large plant where birds nest in its branches. A small amount of yeast works its way through an enormous batch of dough until the whole thing is leavened.

The kingdom starts small. Embarrassingly small. A wandering teacher with a handful of unimpressive followers in a backwater province of the Roman Empire. But give it time.

TREASURE, PEARLS, AND NETS

The final batch of parables zeroes in on the value of the kingdom and the certainty of final judgment.

The parables of the hidden treasure and the pearl of great price are short and punchy. A man finds a treasure buried in a field and sells everything he owns to buy that field. A merchant finds a pearl so valuable that he liquidates his entire business to purchase it. Both stories make the same point: the kingdom is worth everything. When you truly see what it is, you don't haggle. You don't try to get it at a discount. You go all in.

The parable of the net works like the parable of the weeds. Fishermen drag a large net through the Sea of Galilee and catch all kinds of fish. When they pull it to shore, they sort the catch. The good fish go into baskets. The bad ones get thrown away. Just like with the weeds, the separation happens at the end, not in the middle.

Jesus asks his disciples if they understand all of this. They say yes (though the rest of Matthew's story will show they didn't understand as much as they thought). Then Jesus closes with a final image: every teacher who has been trained for the kingdom is like a homeowner who brings out of storage both new treasures and old ones. The kingdom isn't about throwing out the Old Testament and starting over. It's about seeing how everything God has been doing, old and new, fits together in Jesus.

WHAT THIS MEANS FOR US

First, religious rules without compassion miss the point. The Pharisees knew the Bible inside and out, but they used it as a weapon instead of a window. Jesus said God desires mercy, not sacrifice. If your faith makes you less compassionate, something has gone wrong.

Second, the kingdom is hidden but real. It doesn't arrive with fireworks and fanfare. It starts like a seed, like yeast, like a treasure buried in a field. If you're looking for a kingdom that impresses the world right now, you'll miss it. The kingdom works quietly, and it works from the inside out.

Third, not everyone who hears will respond. That's not failure. It's reality. Jesus told the parable of the soils knowing that most ground would be unproductive. What matters is being the good soil: hearing, understanding, and living it out.

Fourth, the kingdom is worth everything. The man who found the treasure didn't resent selling everything he had. He did it with joy. When you see what the kingdom really is, the cost doesn't feel like a sacrifice. It feels like the deal of a lifetime.

TALKING POINTS

1. **The Pharisees saw Jesus heal a man and responded by plotting to kill him.** How does that happen? What makes religious people sometimes resist the very things God is doing?

2. **Jesus said the kingdom is like a mustard seed that starts tiny and grows huge.** Where do you see the kingdom working in small, hidden ways today?

3. **Jesus said that some seed fell among thorns, which represented the worries of life and the desire for other things crowding out God's word.** What kind of "thorns" might choke out someone's faith at your age? What does "good soil" look like practically?

4. The Pharisees accused Jesus of working by Satan's power. Jesus said that attributing God's work to the devil was the most dangerous kind of rejection. Why is that so serious?

5. **The hidden treasure and the pearl both required someone to give up everything.** What would it look like for someone your age to treat the kingdom as worth everything?

The battle lines are drawn. The religious leaders have made their choice, and it's not going to get better from here. But Jesus isn't worried. He knows the kingdom doesn't depend on their approval. It works like seed in soil, like yeast in dough, like treasure waiting to be found. The question isn't whether the kingdom will prevail. The question is who will be paying attention when it does.

Turn the page.

7

WHO DO YOU THINK I AM?

In *The Princess Diaries*, Mia Thermopolis is just an awkward, invisible teenager trying to survive high school in San Francisco. Then one day her grandmother shows up and drops a bombshell: Mia is actually the princess of a small European country called Genovia. She's royalty. She has been all along.

Here's the thing: nobody at her school believes it. They've known Mia for years. They've seen her trip over her own feet, frizz out her hair, and eat lunch alone. A princess? Her? No way. They think they know who she is, and what they know doesn't match.

That's exactly the problem Jesus faces in Matthew 13:54–16:20. Everyone has an opinion about who he is. His hometown thinks he's just a carpenter's kid. Herod thinks he's a dead prophet come back to life. The Pharisees think he's a fraud. The crowds think he's impressive but can't quite figure him out. Even his own disciples are slow to connect the dots.

The question of Jesus' identity has been simmering beneath the surface of Matthew's Gospel since chapter 1. Now it finally boils over. And the answer, when it comes, changes everything.

THE HOMETOWN THAT COULDN'T BELIEVE

Jesus returns to Nazareth, the tiny village where he grew up. He teaches in the local synagogue, and the people are amazed at his wisdom and his reported miracles. But their amazement quickly curdles into suspicion. They start asking questions that sound more like accusations. Isn't this the carpenter's son? Don't we know his mother Mary? Aren't his brothers and sisters still living here among us? Where does this guy get off acting like he's somebody special?

The problem wasn't a lack of evidence. They acknowledged his wisdom and his power. The problem was that they thought they already knew him. They had watched him grow up, play in the streets, learn his father's trade. A boy from Nazareth couldn't be anything more than a boy from Nazareth. Familiarity had blinded them.

Jesus responds with a saying that was probably already well known: a prophet is not without honor except in his hometown and his own house. And then Matthew adds a devastating detail: Jesus did not do many miracles there because of their lack of faith. Not because he couldn't. Because they wouldn't believe.

There's a warning here that still stings. The people closest to the truth are sometimes the least likely to recognize it. Growing up around God's Word, attending church every week, knowing all the Bible stories—none of that automatically produces faith. It can actually work the other way. You can get so used to Jesus that you stop being amazed by him.

A PROPHET MURDERED AT A PARTY

The scene shifts to a dark and disturbing story. Herod Antipas, the ruler of Galilee, hears reports about Jesus and jumps to a panicked conclusion: this must be John the Baptist, raised from the dead.

Why is Herod so rattled? Because he's the one who killed John. Matthew flashes back to explain what happened. John had publicly confronted Herod for marrying Herodias, his brother Philip's wife. This was a clear violation of the law of Moses, and John said so out loud. Herodias wanted John dead for it. Herod was more cautious, partly because he feared John's popularity with the crowds, but he had John arrested and thrown into prison.

Then came Herod's birthday party. Herodias' daughter danced for the guests, and Herod was so pleased that he made a foolish oath: he promised to give her whatever she asked for. Coached by her mother, the girl asked for the head of John the Baptist on a platter.

Herod was distressed, but he was more afraid of looking weak in front of his dinner guests than he was of committing murder. So he gave the order. John was beheaded in prison, and his head was delivered on a dish at a banquet.

It's a horrifying story, and Matthew tells it for a reason. John's fate foreshadows what will happen to Jesus. If the prophet who prepared the way was murdered by a cowardly ruler, what does that tell you about what's coming for the King himself? And if the people closest to power can be this blind and this brutal, the kingdom of God is clearly not going to arrive through political channels.

John's disciples came and buried the body. Then they went and told Jesus. The forerunner's work was finished. The rest belonged to the one he'd been pointing to all along.

TWO FEEDINGS AND A WALK ON WATER

After hearing about John's death, Jesus withdraws by boat to a remote place. But the crowds follow him on foot. When he sees them, he feels deep compassion and heals their sick.

As evening approaches, the disciples want to send the crowds away to buy food in nearby villages. Jesus tells them not to. "You give them something to eat," he says. The disciples are baffled. All they can find is five loaves of bread and two fish. For a crowd of about five thousand men, plus women and children, that's laughable.

But Jesus takes what they have, looks up to heaven, gives thanks, breaks the bread, and hands it to the disciples to distribute. Everyone eats until they're full, and the leftovers fill twelve baskets. Twelve. One for each disciple who thought it couldn't be done.

This miracle echoes the Old Testament in powerful ways. God fed Israel with manna in the wilderness after the exodus from Egypt. The prophet Elisha multiplied bread to feed a hundred men. Now Jesus feeds thousands in a deserted place, doing what only God and his greatest prophets had done before. The kingdom isn't just being talked about. It's being demonstrated with bread in people's hands.

That same night, Jesus sends the disciples ahead by boat across the lake and goes up a mountain to pray alone. A storm hits, and the boat is battered by waves. Then, in the dark hours before dawn, Jesus comes to them walking on the water.

The disciples are terrified. They think he's a ghost. Jesus calls out to them: "Take courage. It is I. Don't be afraid."

Peter, being Peter, asks if he can come out on the water too. Jesus says come. Peter steps out of the boat and actually walks on the water toward Jesus. But when he notices the wind, he panics and starts to sink. Jesus reaches out, catches him, and says, "You of little faith, why did you doubt?"

When they climb into the boat, the wind dies down, and the disciples worship Jesus. They say something they have never said quite this clearly before: "Truly you are the Son of God."

Walking on water isn't just a cool trick. In the Old Testament, control over the sea belongs to God alone. The psalms celebrate God as the one who treads on the waves, who commands the storms, who rules the chaos of the deep. When Jesus walks across the lake in the middle of a storm, he is doing something that Scripture says only God can do. The disciples are starting to see it. They just aren't sure what to do with what they're seeing.

THE REAL SOURCE OF UNCLEANNESS

Back on land, the conflicts with the religious leaders pick up right where they left off. Pharisees and teachers of the law come all the way from Jerusalem to confront Jesus. Their complaint? His disciples don't wash their hands before eating.

This wasn't about hygiene. It was about ritual purity. The Pharisees had developed an elaborate tradition of hand-washing rules based on practices originally designed for priests serving in the temple. They believed these traditions protected the holiness of God's law.

Jesus doesn't defend his disciples' table manners. Instead, he goes on the offensive. He points out that the Pharisees' own traditions sometimes lead them to violate God's actual commands. He gives a specific example: a person could declare their money as a gift dedicated to God and then use that declaration as an excuse not to financially support their aging parents. Their tradition allowed people to dodge the commandment to honor your father and mother. Then Jesus quotes the prophet Isaiah against them: these people honor God with their lips, but their hearts are far from him.

Then Jesus turns to the crowds with a principle that cuts through centuries of purity regulations. What goes into your mouth doesn't make you unclean before God. What comes out of your mouth does. Because what comes out of your mouth comes from your heart. And from the heart come evil thoughts, murder, adultery, theft, lying, and slander. That's what defiles a person. Not unwashed hands.

Jesus isn't abolishing the Old Testament. He's showing what it has always been about. God has always been more interested in the condition of your heart than in the performance of your rituals.

A CANAANITE WOMAN'S ASTONISHING FAITH

Jesus withdraws to the region of Tyre and Sidon, Gentile territory along the Mediterranean coast. A local woman approaches him, crying out for help. Her daughter is tormented by a demon. And she addresses Jesus with a Jewish title: "Lord, Son of David."

At first, Jesus doesn't answer her at all. The disciples want him to send her away because she keeps shouting after them.

When Jesus does speak, he says he was sent only to the lost sheep of Israel.

The woman isn't deterred. She falls at his feet and begs, "Lord, help me."

Jesus responds with what sounds like a harsh comparison: it isn't right to take the children's bread and throw it to the dogs. In Jewish culture, "dogs" was sometimes used as a dismissive label for Gentiles. But the word Jesus uses refers to household dogs, pets that live under the family table, not wild strays.

The woman seizes on this. "Yes, Lord," she says, "but even the house dogs eat the crumbs that fall from their master's table."

Jesus' response is immediate and warm. He tells her that her faith is great, and her daughter is healed at that very moment.

This encounter is one of the most remarkable in the whole Gospel. A Gentile woman, with no claim on Israel's Messiah, shows more faith than almost anyone Jesus has encountered among his own people. She reminds us of the centurion back in chapter 8 whose faith astonished Jesus. These outsiders keep upstaging the insiders. And every time it happens, it previews the mission to the nations that Jesus will command after his resurrection.

Shortly after this, Jesus returns to the Sea of Galilee, heals crowds of people, and performs a second feeding miracle. This time he feeds four thousand men (plus women and children) with seven loaves of bread and a few small fish, with seven baskets of leftovers. Two massive feedings, and the disciples still struggle to trust that Jesus can provide.

SIGNS THEY REFUSE TO SEE

The Pharisees and Sadducees, two groups that normally

disagree about almost everything, team up to test Jesus. They demand a sign from heaven. Something unmistakable. Something in the sky.

Jesus' response is biting. You can read the weather by looking at the sky, he tells them. A red sky at night means fair weather. A red sky in the morning means storms. You know how to interpret the sky, but you can't interpret the signs of the times? The only sign this wicked generation will receive is the sign of Jonah. He's pointing again to his coming death and resurrection, but they aren't listening.

After Jesus leaves them, he warns the disciples to beware of the yeast of the Pharisees and Sadducees. The disciples, who have forgotten to bring bread, think he's talking about actual yeast. Jesus is exasperated. Don't you remember the five thousand? The four thousand? The twelve baskets? The seven baskets? I'm not talking about bread!

He's warning them about the influence of the religious leaders' teaching, their skepticism and hostility, which spreads like yeast through dough. Even a small amount of that kind of cynicism can corrupt everything it touches.

The disciples finally understand. But their slowness is a theme Matthew keeps returning to. These are the people who have had a front-row seat to everything Jesus has done, and they still struggle to see clearly. That should make us patient with our own slowness to understand.

THE CONFESSION THAT CHANGES EVERYTHING

Now comes the turning point. Jesus takes his disciples north to Caesarea Philippi, a thoroughly pagan area near the source of the Jordan River, famous for its shrine to the Greek god Pan. It's about as far from the Jerusalem temple as you can get, both geographically and spiritually. And it's here, in the shadow of pagan religion, that Jesus asks the most important question in the Gospel.

"Who do people say the Son of Man is?"

The disciples report the rumors. Some say John the Baptist. Others say Elijah. Others say Jeremiah or one of the prophets. All respectable answers. All wrong.

Then Jesus makes it personal. "But what about you? Who do you say I am?"

Peter answers: "You are the Christ, the Son of the living God."

This is the moment Matthew has been building toward since the genealogy in chapter 1. Peter doesn't just call Jesus a good teacher or a powerful prophet. He identifies him as the Messiah, God's anointed King, the one Israel has been waiting for, and the Son of the living God.

Jesus tells Peter that flesh and blood didn't reveal this to him. This understanding came from the Father in heaven. Then Jesus makes a series of stunning promises. He calls Peter's confession the thing on which he will build his church, and he says the gates of death will not overpower it. He gives the apostles the keys of the kingdom of heaven and the authority to bind and loose what has already been bound and loosed in heaven, meaning they are to teach God's will to God's people.

Then Jesus tells the disciples not to tell anyone that he is the Christ. Why the secrecy? Because nobody yet understands what kind of Messiah he is. They're expecting a military conqueror who will overthrow Rome. Jesus is headed for a cross.

Until the disciples understand that, broadcasting his identity would only cause confusion. The full truth of who Jesus is won't make sense until after the resurrection.

WHAT THIS MEANS FOR US

First, knowing *about* Jesus isn't the same as knowing Jesus. The people of Nazareth had more access to Jesus than anyone on earth, and they rejected him. Familiarity without faith leads nowhere.

Second, God often works through people nobody expects. A Canaanite woman, a Roman centurion, a handful of fishermen. The kingdom doesn't belong to the religiously impressive. It belongs to those who come to Jesus with nothing but desperate faith.

Third, the question Jesus asked Peter is the question that matters most. Not "What do people say?" but "What do you say?" Everyone has to answer for themselves. And the answer determines everything.

Fourth, Jesus is more than a prophet, more than a teacher, more than a miracle worker. He is the Christ, the Son of the living God. That's the foundation the whole story rests on.

TALKING POINTS

1. **The people of Nazareth couldn't believe Jesus was special because they thought they already knew him.** Have you ever been so familiar with something about God or the Bible that you stopped being amazed by it?

2. **When the Canaanite woman begged Jesus to heal her daughter, he was initially silent and then seemed to refuse her.**

Why do you think Jesus tested her before granting her request? What does her persistence teach us about faith?

3. **Peter correctly identified Jesus as the Christ, but Jesus said this knowledge came from God, not from human reasoning.** What does that tell us about how people come to understand who Jesus really is?

4. **Jesus fed thousands of people twice, and the disciples still worried about not having enough bread.** Why is it so hard to trust God even after he's already provided?

5. **Jesus asked his disciples point-blank, "Who do you say I am?"** If someone asked you, "Who do you think Jesus is?" what would you say? How would you explain it?

The question has finally been answered. Jesus is the Christ, the Son of the living God. But knowing who he is and understanding what that means are two very different things. Peter got the title right, but he doesn't yet understand the mission. Because the Messiah everyone expected would wear a crown. The Messiah nobody expected would carry a cross.

Turn the page.

8

THE KING NOBODY WANTED

In the original *Star Wars* trilogy, Luke Skywalker spends the first two movies dreaming about becoming a Jedi, defeating the Empire, and saving the galaxy. He imagines lightsaber battles and heroic victories. Then in *The Empire Strikes Back*, his training with Yoda takes a hard turn. The path of a Jedi isn't glory and excitement. It's patience, sacrifice, and suffering. And the worst moment of all comes when Luke discovers the villain he's been fighting is his own father. The story he thought he was living in turns out to be a completely different kind of story.

Something similar happens to the disciples in Matthew 16:21–18:35. Peter has just made the greatest confession of the Gospel: Jesus is the Christ, the Son of the living God. The disciples think they know where this is heading. The Messiah will take his throne, defeat his enemies, and restore Israel's glory. Finally, it's all going to pay off.

Then Jesus drops a bomb. He's not heading for a throne. He's heading for a cross.

These chapters cover the most dramatic turn in Matthew's story. The disciples learn that the Messiah they confessed must die, that following him means dying too, and that the greatest in his kingdom are not the powerful but the humble. Everything they thought they understood about the kingdom gets turned upside down. Again.

THE CROSS NOBODY SAW COMING

Right after Peter's confession, Matthew writes a sentence that changes the direction of the entire Gospel: "From that time on Jesus began to explain to his disciples that he must go to Jerusalem and suffer many things at the hands of the elders, chief priests and teachers of the law, and that he must be killed and on the third day be raised to life." *Must.* Not might. Not could. Must.

This is the first time Jesus has spoken this plainly about what's ahead. There have been hints before. He's talked about his "hour" and compared himself to Jonah spending three days in the belly of the great fish. But now there's no ambiguity. He's going to Jerusalem. The religious leaders are going to kill him. And on the third day, he'll rise again.

Peter's reaction is immediate. He pulls Jesus aside and rebukes him. "Never, Lord! This shall never happen to you!" You can almost hear the panic in his voice. He just declared Jesus to be the Messiah. The Messiah doesn't die. The Messiah wins.

Jesus' response is one of the most shocking lines in the Gospel. He turns to Peter and says, "Get behind me, Satan! You are a stumbling block to me; you do not have in mind the concerns of God, but merely human concerns."

Satan. Jesus calls Peter Satan. Not because Peter is evil, but because Peter is doing exactly what Satan did in the wilderness. In chapter 4, the devil offered Jesus the kingdoms of the world without the cross. Now Peter is offering the same deal: a crown without suffering, a throne without a cross. It's the most attractive temptation in the world, and Jesus refuses it flat.

The disciple who was just called the rock on which Jesus would build his church has become a stumbling block. That's how fast someone can go from speaking for God to speaking for the devil, simply by replacing God's agenda with their own comfort.

IF ANYONE WOULD FOLLOW ME

Then Jesus turns to all the disciples and lays down the terms of following him. Anyone who wants to come after him must deny themselves, take up their cross, and follow him.

In the Roman world, "taking up your cross" was not a metaphor for dealing with minor inconveniences. It meant one thing: walking to your own execution. Condemned criminals carried the horizontal beam of their cross through the streets to the place where they would be nailed to it and left to die. Jesus is telling his followers that the road ahead leads through death, not around it.

Then comes the paradox that sits at the heart of the Gospel: whoever wants to save their life will lose it, but whoever loses their life for Jesus' sake will find it. What good is it if you gain everything the world offers but lose your own soul? What could you possibly trade for your soul?

Jesus isn't asking people to be miserable for the sake of being miserable. He's saying that clinging to this life as if it's all there is will cost you everything that actually matters. But letting go of this life for the sake of Jesus and his kingdom opens the door to something that can never be taken away.

He closes with a promise: the Son of Man is going to come in his Father's glory with his angels, and he will repay everyone according to what they have done. The suffering is real. But it's not the end of the story.

A GLIMPSE OF GLORY

Six days later, Jesus takes Peter, James, and John up a high mountain. And there, something happens that none of them will ever forget.

Jesus is transfigured before their eyes. His face shines like the sun. His clothes become as white as light. And standing with him, talking with him, are Moses and Elijah, two of the greatest figures in all of Israel's history. Moses represents the Law. Elijah represents the Prophets. Together, they represent everything God has been doing since the beginning. And they are standing with Jesus, as if the entire Old Testament has been pointing to this moment.

Peter, overwhelmed, blurts out an offer to build three shelters, one for Jesus, one for Moses, and one for Elijah. He wants to freeze the moment, to stay on the mountain where everything is glorious and no one is talking about crosses.

But while Peter is still talking, a bright cloud covers them, and a voice speaks from it. The same voice that spoke at Jesus' baptism now speaks again: "This is my Son, whom I love; with him I am well pleased. Listen to him!"

Listen to him. Even when he's talking about suffering and death. Even when his words don't match your expectations. Listen to him.

When the cloud lifts, Moses and Elijah are gone. Only

Jesus remains. And that's the point. The Law and the Prophets are important, but they were always pointing to Jesus. He's the one who matters most. He's the one to follow.

As they come down the mountain, Jesus tells them not to tell anyone what they've seen until after the Son of Man has been raised from the dead. Why? Because the transfiguration only makes sense in light of the resurrection. Until Jesus has died and risen, even a glimpse of his glory could be misunderstood. People would want the glory without the cross, just like Peter did.

The disciples ask about the Jewish belief that Elijah must come before the Messiah. Jesus confirms it and tells them Elijah has already come, but they didn't recognize him. Matthew makes clear that Jesus is talking about John the Baptist. Elijah came, and they killed him. And the Son of Man will suffer in the same way.

FAITH THE SIZE OF A MUSTARD SEED

Back at the bottom of the mountain, reality is waiting. A man approaches Jesus because the remaining disciples couldn't heal his son, who was tormented by a demon that caused violent seizures. The boy kept falling into fire and water.

Jesus heals the boy instantly. When the disciples ask privately why they couldn't do it, Jesus' answer is direct: because of their little faith. Then he adds that if they had faith even as small as a mustard seed, they could tell a mountain to move and it would move. Nothing would be impossible.

This is humbling. Jesus had already given these disciples authority over demons back in chapter 10. They had been successful before. But somewhere between then and now, their trust had shrunk. They were relying on their own experience or their own techniques instead of actively depending on God.

Jesus then predicts his death a second time. The Son of Man is going to be delivered into the hands of men. They will kill him. And on the third day he will be raised. Matthew tells us the disciples were filled with grief. They're starting to hear it, even if they can't fully understand it yet.

THE TEMPLE TAX AND A FISH

A brief, quirky scene follows. Tax collectors approach Peter and ask if Jesus pays the temple tax, a small annual fee every Jewish man paid for the upkeep of the temple in Jerusalem. Peter says yes.

When Peter comes inside, Jesus gets ahead of him with a question. Do kings collect taxes from their own children, or from other people? From other people, Peter answers. Then the children are exempt, Jesus says.

The point is subtle but important. If the temple belongs to God, and Jesus is God's Son, then technically Jesus doesn't owe the tax. But Jesus tells Peter to go catch a fish, and in its mouth he'll find a coin worth enough to pay the tax for both of them. Jesus pays it anyway, not because he has to, but because he doesn't want to cause an unnecessary offense.

This is a small picture of a big principle. Jesus doesn't insist on his rights when doing so would distract from his mission. His followers should think the same way.

WHO IS THE GREATEST?

Chapter 18 opens with a question the disciples apparently couldn't stop thinking about: who is the greatest in the kingdom of heaven? They've been traveling with the king. They've seen the glory on the mountain. Naturally, they want to know who gets the best seat.

Jesus' answer demolishes their assumptions. He calls a small child over, stands the child in the middle of the group, and tells them that unless they turn and become like little children, they will never enter the kingdom of heaven. The greatest in the kingdom is whoever humbles themselves like this child.

In Jesus' culture, children had virtually no social status. They couldn't earn money, hold positions, or demand respect. They were completely dependent on others. And that, Jesus says, is the model for kingdom greatness. Not ambition. Not achievement. Not influence. Dependence. Humility. The willingness to be small.

Then Jesus adds that whoever welcomes a little child in his name welcomes him. The way you treat the people with the least power and the least status is the way you're treating Jesus.

MILLSTONES, LOST SHEEP, AND TOUGH LOVE

Jesus continues with a series of warnings and instructions about life in the community of his followers.

First, a terrifying warning: if anyone causes one of these little ones who believe in him to stumble, it would be better for that person to have a massive millstone hung around their neck and be drowned in the sea. The millstone Jesus describes isn't the small kind a woman would use at home. It's the heavy stone turned by a donkey. Jesus is saying that leading a vulnerable believer away from the faith is such a serious offense that a violent death would actually be the lighter punishment compared to what God has in store.

Next, Jesus tells the parable of the lost sheep. A shepherd has a hundred sheep and one wanders off. Does he leave the ninety-nine on the hills and go search for the one? Of course he does. And when he finds it, he's happier about that one than about the ninety-nine that stayed put. God doesn't want even one of his little ones to be lost.

Then Jesus outlines what to do when a fellow believer sins against you. The process is careful and gradual. First, go to the person privately. If they listen, you've won them back. If they don't, bring one or two others as witnesses. If they still refuse to listen, bring it before the whole church. And if they reject even the church, treat them as an outsider.

This is tough love, not cruelty. The goal at every step is restoration, not punishment. You start private and go public only when necessary. And the whole process is wrapped in the promise that where two or three gather in Jesus' name, he is there with them. The church doesn't act alone in these matters. Jesus is present, guiding the process.

THE PARABLE THAT DROPS THE MIC

Peter approaches Jesus with a question that sounds generous: "Lord, how many times should I forgive my brother or sister who sins against me? Up to seven times?" Some Jewish teachers suggested forgiving three times was enough. Peter doubles it and adds one. He probably expects a pat on the back.

Jesus says, "Not seven times, but seventy-seven times." (Some translations say "seventy times seven.") Either way, the point isn't a specific number. The point is that you stop counting.

Then Jesus tells a parable to explain why. A king decides to settle accounts with his servants. One servant owes him ten thousand talents. This is a staggering number, almost comically huge. Ten thousand was the largest number used in ordinary speech, and a talent was the largest unit of currency. The combined annual tax revenue of Galilee and Perea was only about two hundred talents. This servant owes a debt that could never be repaid in a thousand lifetimes.

The servant begs for mercy, and the king does something astonishing: he forgives the entire debt. Every last coin. Gone.

But then that same servant goes out and finds a fellow servant who owes him a hundred denarii. It's a real debt, but compared to what he just had canceled, it's pocket change. Instead of showing the same mercy he received, he grabs the man by the throat and has him thrown into prison.

When the king hears about it, he is furious. He calls the servant back and hands him over to be tortured until he pays everything he owes, which of course means forever.

Jesus closes the parable with words that should make every listener sit up straight: "This is how my heavenly Father will treat each of you unless you forgive your brother or sister from your heart."

The math of this parable is the math of the Gospel. God has forgiven us a debt so massive it's beyond calculation. Every sin we've ever committed against a holy God has been absorbed by his grace. If we then refuse to forgive the comparatively small offenses other people commit against us, we prove that we never really understood the grace we received.

WHAT THIS MEANS FOR US

First, following Jesus means giving up control. Peter wanted a Messiah without a cross. We often want a faith without sacrifice. But Jesus never offered that deal. He offered himself, and the road to him goes through self-denial.

Second, greatness in the kingdom is measured by how low you're willing to go, not how high you can climb. The child in the middle of the room, not the disciple arguing for the best seat, is the model for kingdom living.

Third, forgiveness isn't optional. It's the evidence that you've understood the Gospel. If you've been forgiven an unpayable debt, you can't refuse to forgive the small debts others owe you.

Fourth, Jesus knows the cross is coming and he walks toward it anyway. That tells you something about his courage. But it also tells you something about his love. He chose the cross because it was the only way to pay the debt we could never pay ourselves.

TALKING POINTS

1. **Jesus called Peter "Satan" one minute after calling him the rock of the church.** What does that teach you about how quickly someone can go from speaking God's truth to speaking against it?

2. **Jesus said you have to lose your life to find it.** What are some ways a person your age might try to "save" their life instead of surrendering it to Jesus?

3. **At the transfiguration, God said, "Listen to him!"** Why do you think it's hard to listen to Jesus when his words are uncomfortable or costly?

4. **Jesus said that whoever welcomes a child in his name welcomes him.** Who are the "little ones" or low-status people in your life? How could you welcome them?

5. **In the parable of the unforgiving servant, the man who was forgiven millions refused to forgive a tiny debt.** Is there someone you're holding a grudge against? What would it look like to forgive them?

The disciples are learning, slowly, that the kingdom of God runs on a completely different operating system than the world. In the world, you climb over others to get to the top. In the kingdom, you kneel down to lift others up. In the world, you protect yourself at all costs. In the kingdom, you lay your life down.

And the king leads the way, walking straight toward a cross that no one else would choose, because that's what love looks like when it refuses to quit.

Turn the page.

9

THE UPSIDE-DOWN KINGDOM

Imagine you're playing a video game where you've been grinding for hours. You've leveled up your character, earned the best gear, and fought your way through the hardest bosses. Then someone walks in, picks up a controller, and the game gives them the exact same rewards you just spent all day earning. They skipped the grind. They didn't fight anything. And the game treats them the same as you.

You'd be furious. That's not fair.

But what if the person who designed the game showed up and said, "I made this game. I get to decide how the rewards work. And I'm being generous, not unfair."

That tension between fairness and generosity, between earning your place and receiving a gift, sits right at the heart of Matthew 19–20. These two chapters read like a series of conversations where Jesus takes everything people assume about status, success, and reward and flips it on its head. The powerful are warned. The weak are welcomed. The first end up last. And the one headed for the throne turns out to be headed for a cross.

Welcome to the upside-down kingdom.

MARRIAGE, DIVORCE, AND HARD HEARTS

Jesus has left Galilee for the last time. He's heading south toward Jerusalem, toward the cross he predicted in chapter 16. Large crowds follow him, and he heals the sick as he goes.

The Pharisees show up with a loaded question: Is it lawful for a man to divorce his wife for any reason at all? This wasn't an innocent question. It was a trap. The two main schools of Pharisaic teaching disagreed sharply about divorce. The school of Shammai said a man could divorce his wife only for sexual unfaithfulness. The school of Hillel said a man could divorce his wife for practically any reason, even something as trivial as burning his dinner. The Pharisees wanted to force Jesus to pick a side so they could turn whichever group he disagreed with against him.

Jesus refuses to play their game. Instead of starting with the passage in Deuteronomy they're fighting about, he goes all the way back to the beginning. Haven't you read, he asks, that the Creator made them male and female? That a man leaves his father and mother and is joined to his wife, and the two become one flesh? What God has joined together, no one should separate.

Jesus isn't just offering an opinion on divorce law. He's going behind the law to the Creator's original design. Marriage was always supposed to be permanent. The "one flesh" language means that marriage creates a bond as deep as a family tie. It isn't a contract you can cancel when things get inconvenient.

The Pharisees push back: then why did Moses command a certificate of divorce? Jesus corrects them sharply. Moses didn't command it. He permitted it. And he only did that because of the hardness of your hearts. Divorce was never part of God's plan. It was an emergency measure for a broken world.

Jesus does allow one exception: divorce in the case of unfaithfulness. When one partner breaks the marriage through infidelity, the bond has already been shattered. But Jesus' overall point is unmistakable. Marriage is sacred, and God's people should fight to protect it, not look for excuses to escape it.

The disciples are so startled by the strictness of Jesus' teaching that they blurt out, "If that's the deal, it's better not to marry!" Jesus doesn't disagree entirely. He acknowledges that some people will remain single for the sake of the kingdom. Singleness isn't a consolation prize. It's a legitimate calling for those God equips for it.

What's quietly radical about this whole conversation is how Jesus protects the vulnerable. In his culture, divorce was almost entirely a man's privilege. A woman had almost no power to protect herself. By tightening the rules, Jesus wasn't being harsh. He was shielding wives from being discarded by husbands with hard hearts.

LET THE CHILDREN COME

Right after this heavy conversation about marriage, people start bringing children to Jesus so he can bless them and pray for them. The disciples try to shoo them away. They've got important kingdom business to discuss. Children can wait.

Jesus is having none of it. Let the children come to me, he says. Don't stop them. The kingdom of heaven belongs to people like these.

This is especially pointed because Jesus just spent chapter 18 teaching the disciples that the greatest in the kingdom are those who humble themselves like children. And here they are, shooing actual children away. They heard the lesson but missed the point.

In Jesus' world, children had virtually no social standing. They couldn't earn, couldn't vote, couldn't contribute anything measurable. They were entirely dependent on others. And that's exactly why Jesus holds them up as models. The kingdom doesn't belong to the impressive. It belongs to those who know they need help.

THE RICH MAN WHO WALKED AWAY

Then comes one of the most unsettling encounters in the entire Gospel. A young man approaches Jesus and asks a question that sounds sincere: "Teacher, what good thing must I do to gain eternal life?"

Jesus tells him to keep the commandments. The man asks which ones. Jesus lists several of the Ten Commandments, all of them focused on how you treat other people: don't murder, don't commit adultery, don't steal, don't lie, honor your parents. Then he adds the summary from Leviticus: love your neighbor as yourself.

The young man says he's kept all of these. Then he asks what he still lacks.

This is where the conversation takes a sharp turn. Jesus tells him that if he wants to be complete, he should sell his possessions, give the money to the poor, and come follow Jesus. He'll have treasure in heaven instead.

The young man walks away in grief, because he has many possessions.

Notice what happened. Jesus didn't tell every person he met to sell everything. But he could see that this particular man's wealth had become his real master. The man wanted eternal life, but he didn't want it more than he wanted his comfortable life. He wanted a teacher who would affirm him, not a Lord who would demand sacrifice. And when the cost became clear, he chose his stuff over the kingdom.

After the man leaves, Jesus turns to the disciples and says it is easier for a camel to go through the eye of a needle than for a rich person to enter the kingdom of God. This is deliberate exaggeration to make a point that can't be missed. Wealth gives you the illusion that you don't need anyone, including God. It makes you feel secure, independent, and in control. And those feelings are the exact opposite of the childlike dependence Jesus just said the kingdom requires.

The disciples are stunned. In their culture, wealth was often seen as a sign of God's blessing. If the rich can't be saved, who can?

Jesus' answer is both sobering and hopeful: with human beings this is impossible, but with God all things are possible. Salvation isn't something anyone can earn, rich or poor. It's a gift from God. But you have to be willing to let go of whatever you're gripping tighter than you're gripping him.

WHAT DO WE GET?

Peter, ever the spokesman, pipes up with the question the other disciples are probably thinking: "We've left everything to follow you. What will we get?" It's an honest question. Maybe not the most noble question, but honest.

Jesus doesn't scold him for asking. He promises that in the age of renewal, when the Son of Man sits on his glorious throne, the twelve disciples will sit on twelve thrones judging the twelve tribes of Israel. And anyone who has left homes, family, or property for Jesus' sake will receive a hundred times as much and will inherit eternal life.

Jesus validates sacrifice. Following him costs something real, and he doesn't pretend otherwise. But the return on investment is beyond calculation. Not just in the future, but in the present, where the community of believers becomes a new family that shares life and resources together.

Then Jesus adds a warning that frames everything that follows: "Many who are first will be last, and the last will be first."

Don't get comfortable. Don't assume your position is secure just because you showed up early. The kingdom runs on different math.

THE WORKERS AND THE GENEROUS LANDOWNER

To drive this point home, Jesus tells one of his most provocative parables. A landowner goes out early in the morning to hire workers for his vineyard. He agrees to pay them a denarius, the standard daily wage. A few hours later, he goes back and hires more workers, promising to pay them whatever is fair. He does the same at noon and in the afternoon. Then, with only one hour left in the workday, he hires a final group who have been standing around all day because nobody hired them.

When evening comes, the landowner pays the last group first, and he gives them a full denarius. The workers who started at dawn see this and naturally expect more. But when their turn comes, they also receive one denarius. Exactly what they were promised.

They're furious. "These last workers only put in one hour, and you've made them equal to us! We've been out here all day in the blazing heat!"

The landowner responds calmly: "Friend, I'm not being unfair to you. Didn't you agree to work for a denarius? I have the right to do what I want with my own money. Or are you envious because I am generous?"

This parable isn't about employment law. It's about God. God's generosity doesn't operate on a merit system. He doesn't owe anyone more because they showed up earlier or worked harder. Everyone in the vineyard gets more than they deserve. The problem isn't that the early workers were cheated. They weren't. The problem is that they couldn't stand watching someone else receive the same grace they did without "earning" it.

This is one of the hardest truths about the kingdom: grace offends people who think they've earned their place. If you've been following God your whole life, it can sting to watch someone come to faith at the last minute and receive the same welcome. But that sting reveals something about your heart. It means you've started thinking of God's generosity as something you deserved rather than something you received.

Jesus closes the parable with the same phrase he used before: the last will be first, and the first will be last.

THE THIRD PREDICTION AND A MOTHER'S REQUEST

As they continue toward Jerusalem, Jesus pulls the twelve aside for his third and most detailed prediction of his death. The Son of Man will be handed over to the chief priests and teachers of the law. They will condemn him to death. They will hand him over to the Gentiles, who will mock him, flog him, and crucify him. On the third day, he will be raised.

This is as clear as it gets. Mockery. Flogging. Crucifixion. Resurrection. No metaphors. No riddles.

And what happens immediately afterward? The mother of James and John approaches Jesus, kneels before him, and asks if her two sons can sit at his right and left in his kingdom. The best seats. The highest honor.

It's breathtaking. Jesus has just described his torture and execution, and the response is a request for VIP seating.

Jesus asks James and John directly: can you drink the cup I'm about to drink? In the prophets, "the cup" is an image for suffering and judgment. They answer confidently: "We can." They have no idea what they're agreeing to. Jesus tells them they will indeed drink his cup, but the seating arrangements aren't his to give. Those belong to the Father.

The other ten disciples are furious, not because the request was inappropriate, but because they wanted those seats too. This whole group is still thinking about the kingdom in terms of power, rank, and personal advantage.

Jesus gathers them together and delivers a speech that summarizes everything these two chapters have been building toward. The rulers of the world lord their power over people. That's how the world works. But it must not be that way among you. Whoever wants to be great must be a servant. Whoever wants to be first must be a slave. And then the defining statement: "The Son of Man did not come to be served, but to serve, and to give his life as a ransom for many."

This is the first time in Matthew that Jesus explicitly explains the purpose of his death. It's not an accident. It's not a tragedy. It's a ransom, a price paid to set people free. And it reveals the deepest truth about God's kingdom: the king himself is the servant. The one with the most power uses it to rescue the people with the least.

TWO BLIND MEN WHO GOT IT RIGHT

The chapter ends with a scene that contrasts beautifully with what just happened. As Jesus leaves Jericho on the road to Jerusalem, two blind beggars sitting by the roadside hear that Jesus is passing by. They cry out, "Have mercy on us, Lord, Son of David!"

The crowd tells them to shut up. They're interrupting. They're insignificant.

The blind men shout louder.

Jesus stops. He asks them what they want. They say, "Lord, we want to see."

Moved with compassion, Jesus touches their eyes. Immediately they can see. And the first thing they do with their new sight is follow him.

James and John came to Jesus asking for thrones. The blind men came asking for mercy. The disciples wanted status. The beggars wanted help. And the beggars got exactly what they needed.

In the upside-down kingdom, that's how it works every single time.

WHAT THIS MEANS FOR US

First, God cares about the vulnerable. Whether it's a wife being unfairly divorced, a child being ignored, or a blind beggar being silenced, Jesus consistently stands with the people everyone else overlooks.

Second, wealth and comfort are more dangerous than most people realize. The rich young man wasn't evil. He was moral, polite, and sincere. But his possessions had a grip on him that he couldn't break. Following Jesus requires open hands.

Third, grace isn't fair, and that's the point. The parable of the workers teaches that God's generosity is determined by his character, not by our performance. If that offends you, it might be because you've been keeping score.

Fourth, true greatness is service. The kingdom doesn't reward people who climb to the top. It rewards people who stoop to help others up.

TALKING POINTS

1. **The rich young man kept all the commandments but walked away when Jesus asked for more.** What are some things people your age might hold onto more tightly than they hold onto Jesus?

2. **The parable of the vineyard workers makes some people uncomfortable.** Does it bother you that everyone got paid the same? Why or why not?

3. Jesus said the rulers of the world lord their power over people, but his followers should be servants. Where do you see people "lording power" over others in your daily life? What would it look like to be a servant instead?

4. The blind men refused to be silenced even when the crowd told them to be quiet. What can we learn from their persistence?

5. Jesus said the first will be last and the last will be first. What does that look like practically in a school, a church, or a friend group?

The road to Jerusalem is getting shorter. The cross is getting closer. And with every step, Jesus keeps teaching the same lesson in different ways: the kingdom of God doesn't work like anything you've ever seen.

The last are first. The servants are the greatest. And the king? The king is on his way to die, not because he lost, but because that's what love does when the price needs to be paid.

Turn the page.

10

THE KING WALKS INTO THE BUILDING

In *The Wizard of Oz*, Dorothy and her friends finally reach the Emerald City. They've traveled a long, dangerous road to get there. They expect that the great and powerful Wizard will solve all their problems. But when they actually meet him, the curtain gets pulled back and everything they assumed turns out to be wrong. The Wizard isn't what anyone expected. And neither is the real power in the room.

Matthew 21–22 are the Emerald City moment in Jesus' story. After chapters of traveling, teaching, healing, and predicting his own death, Jesus finally arrives in Jerusalem. The holy city. The capital. The place where the temple stood, where God's presence was supposed to dwell, where the religious power brokers ran things.

And when Jesus walks through those gates, he pulls back the curtain on everything. He enters like a king, but not the kind anyone wanted. He goes to the temple, but not to worship. He goes to war. Not with swords, but with stories, questions, and an authority that nobody can match.

These two chapters contain some of the most dramatic scenes in the entire Gospel. A parade. A protest. A withered tree. Three parables aimed like arrows at the religious leaders. And four trap questions that Jesus dodges so brilliantly that no one dares ask him anything ever again.

THE KING RIDES IN ON A DONKEY

As Jesus approaches Jerusalem from the east, he sends two disciples ahead to get a donkey and its colt. He tells them exactly where the animals will be and exactly what to say if anyone asks questions. Everything goes just as he described.

Matthew wants his readers to know this isn't random. He points back to the prophet Zechariah, who wrote centuries earlier that Israel's king would come to Jerusalem "gentle and riding on a donkey." In the ancient world, a king riding a horse meant war. A king riding a donkey meant peace. By choosing a donkey, Jesus is making a public declaration: he is the promised king, but not a military conqueror. He is the meek one.

The crowd doesn't seem to catch the distinction. As Jesus rides toward the city, people go wild. They spread their cloaks on the road and cut tree branches to lay before him, the ancient version of rolling out a red carpet. They shout words from Psalm 118: "Hosanna to the Son of David! Blessed is he who comes in the name of the Lord!"

It looks like a victory parade. The problem is that it's being thrown by people who misunderstand the victory. They want a political liberator who will overthrow Rome. Jesus is heading to a cross. When the whole city buzzes with the question "Who is this?", the Galilean pilgrims answer, "This is the prophet Jesus, from Nazareth in Galilee." True, but nowhere close to the full truth.

OVERTURNING TABLES

Jesus goes straight to the temple, and what he does there shocks everyone. He drives out the people buying and selling animals for sacrifice. He flips over the tables of the money changers and the benches of the dove sellers. Then he says, quoting Isaiah and Jeremiah: "My house will be called a house of prayer, but you are making it a den of robbers."

This wasn't a spontaneous outburst. It was a deliberate prophetic action. The buying and selling happened in the outer court of the temple, the only area where non-Jewish people were allowed to come and pray. By filling it with a marketplace, the temple leaders had essentially turned the Gentiles' worship space into a shopping mall. The temple was supposed to be a house of prayer for all nations. Instead it had become a place where the powerful profited and the outsiders got squeezed out.

By quoting Jeremiah 7, Jesus was making a terrifying comparison. In Jeremiah's day, the people of Judah assumed the temple would protect them from God's judgment no matter how they behaved. Jeremiah warned them they were wrong, and Jerusalem was destroyed. Jesus is warning that history is about to repeat itself.

After clearing out the merchants, Jesus heals blind and lame people who come to him in the temple. Children begin shouting, "Hosanna to the Son of David!" The chief priests and teachers of the law are furious. Jesus responds by quoting Psalm 8: out of the mouths of children, God has called forth praise.

The contrast is sharp. The religious leaders are outraged. The children get it right. The people with the most education and authority miss the truth, while the people with the least status see it clearly.

THE FIG TREE AND A LESSON ON FAITH

The next morning, heading back to Jerusalem, Jesus sees a fig tree covered in leaves but bearing no fruit. He tells the tree it will never bear fruit again, and it withers immediately. The disciples are stunned.

This isn't Jesus being angry at a plant. It's an acted-out parable. In the Old Testament, Israel was often compared to a fig tree or a vineyard, and a fruitless tree symbolized a nation that looked alive on the outside but had nothing real to offer. Jesus had just walked into the temple and found the same thing: all the outward show of religion but no genuine fruit of faithfulness, justice, or mercy.

When the disciples ask how the tree withered so quickly, Jesus turns it into a lesson about faith. If they have faith and don't doubt, they could even tell "this mountain" to throw itself into the sea. Since they were looking directly at the Temple Mount as he said this, the lesson carried an extra edge. The temple system that had become fruitless would be removed, and a new way of approaching God through faith and prayer would take its place.

THREE PARABLES THAT HIT HARD

When Jesus returns to the temple, the chief priests and elders confront him. By what authority are you doing these things?

Who gave you this authority?

Jesus answers with a counter-question: Was John the Baptist's ministry from heaven or from human beings? The leaders huddle and realize they're trapped. If they say "from heaven," Jesus will ask why they didn't believe John. If they say "from human beings," the crowd will turn on them because everyone considered John a prophet. So they mumble, "We don't know." Jesus responds: then I won't tell you by what authority I do these things, either.

Having exposed their dishonesty, Jesus tells three parables in a row, each one aimed directly at the religious leaders. Together, these parables form an indictment, a verdict, and a warning.

The Two Sons. A father asks two sons to work in his vineyard. The first says no but later changes his mind and goes. The second says yes but never shows up. Which one did the father's will? Obviously the first. Jesus tells the leaders that tax collectors and prostitutes are entering the kingdom of God ahead of them, because those notorious sinners actually repented when John preached, while the leaders, who said all the right religious words, never changed a thing. In the kingdom, what you do matters more than what you promise.

The Wicked Tenants. A landowner plants a vineyard, sets it up with everything it needs, and rents it to tenant farmers before going on a journey. When he sends servants to collect his share of the harvest, the tenants beat them, stone them, and kill them. He sends more servants. Same result. Finally he sends his own son, thinking the tenants will respect him. Instead, they drag the son outside the vineyard and kill him.

Jesus asks: what will the landowner do to those tenants? The answer is obvious. He'll destroy them and give the vineyard to others who will actually produce fruit.

The vineyard is Israel. The tenants are the religious leaders. The servants are the prophets God sent throughout Israel's history, who were consistently rejected and persecuted. The son is Jesus himself. And the warning is devastating: the kingdom of God will be taken from you and given to a people who produce its fruit.

The leaders realize Jesus is talking about them. They want to arrest him but are afraid of the crowds, who still consider Jesus a prophet.

The Wedding Banquet. A king throws a wedding feast for his son and sends servants to invite the guests. The invited guests refuse to come. He sends more servants with an even more generous description of the feast. Some ignore the invitation. Others seize the servants and kill them. The king is furious and sends his army to destroy their city. Then he tells his servants to go out to the streets and invite anyone they can find, good and bad alike. The banquet hall fills up.

But when the king enters the hall, he spots a man not wearing wedding clothes. He asks how the man got in without proper attire. The man has nothing to say. The king has him thrown into the outer darkness.

This parable has two warnings packed into one. The first is for the religious leaders who rejected God's invitation through Jesus. They had every advantage, every reason to respond, and they refused. So the invitation went out to everyone else, including the most unlikely people. The second warning is for those who accept the invitation but treat it casually. Coming to the feast isn't enough. You have to take it seriously. You can't receive God's grace and then act as if it doesn't matter. The parable ends with the chilling line: many are invited, but few are chosen.

FOUR TRAPS THAT ALL BACKFIRE

Having failed to discredit Jesus with direct challenges, the various groups of leaders now send wave after wave of trick questions, hoping to catch him in a statement they can use against him.

Trap 1: Taxes to Caesar. The Pharisees team up with the Herodians, a group loyal to the ruling family of Herod. Normally these two parties can't stand each other, but Jesus is enough of a threat to make them temporary allies. They ask: Is it lawful to pay taxes to Caesar, or not?

It's a brilliant trap. If Jesus says yes, the crowd will see him as a Roman collaborator and lose faith in him as the Messiah. If Jesus says no, the Herodians will report him to the Roman authorities as a rebel.

Jesus asks to see a coin. Whose image is on it? Caesar's, they answer. Then give to Caesar what belongs to Caesar, Jesus says, and give to God what belongs to God.

The answer is stunning in its simplicity. Yes, governments have legitimate authority and citizens have real obligations. But that authority is limited. God's claim on your life is total. The coin bears Caesar's image, but every human being bears God's image. Give Caesar his coins. Give God your whole self.

His opponents are so amazed they just walk away.

Trap 2: The Resurrection Riddle. Next come the Sadducees, the wealthy priestly party who didn't believe in the resurrection of the dead. They pose a hypothetical scenario designed to make the idea of resurrection look absurd. A woman marries seven brothers in succession (each dying before producing children, following the Old Testament law that required a brother to marry his deceased brother's widow). In the resurrection, whose wife will she be?

Jesus tells them they're wrong on two counts. They don't know the Scriptures, and they don't know the power of God. In the resurrection, people won't marry. They'll be like angels. The question is based on a false assumption that the next life is just a continuation of this one.

Then Jesus hits them where it hurts. Even in the books of Moses, which the Sadducees accepted as authoritative, God says, "I am the God of Abraham, the God of Isaac, and the God of Jacob." Not "I was." I am. God is the God of the living, not the dead. If God still claims a relationship with these long-dead patriarchs, then they must still be alive in some meaningful sense, and the resurrection is where that relationship reaches its fulfillment.

The crowd is astonished. The Sadducees are silenced.

Trap 3: The Greatest Commandment. The Pharisees regroup and send a legal expert to test Jesus with a question their own scholars debated among themselves: which commandment in the law is the greatest?

Jesus gives an answer that no one can argue with. Love the Lord your God with all your heart, soul, and mind. That's the first and greatest commandment. And the second is like it:

love your neighbor as yourself. Everything in the Law and the Prophets hangs on these two.

By linking love for God and love for neighbor as inseparable, Jesus creates a framework for understanding the entire Old Testament. You can't truly love God without loving the people around you. And you can't properly love people without first being anchored in love for God. Every other commandment is an expression of one or both of these.

Jesus' Counter-Question. Now it's Jesus' turn. He asks the Pharisees: what do you think about the Messiah? Whose son is he? They give the standard answer: the son of David.

Then Jesus quotes Psalm 110, in which David wrote, "The Lord said to my Lord, sit at my right hand until I put your enemies under your feet." If David calls the Messiah "my Lord," how can the Messiah be merely David's descendant? A father doesn't call his own son "Lord." The Messiah must be something greater than just a human king from David's bloodline.

No one can answer. And from that day on, Matthew tells us, nobody dared to ask Jesus any more questions.

The debates are over. Jesus has won every round. But winning the arguments won't save his life. In fact, it's the opposite. By publicly humiliating the most powerful people in Jerusalem, Jesus has guaranteed that they will move against him. The cross is now inevitable.

WHAT THIS MEANS FOR US

First, Jesus enters Jerusalem as king, but he defines kingship on his own terms. He chooses a donkey, not a war horse.

He serves, not conquers. The kind of power Jesus brings looks nothing like the power the world admires.

Second, religious activity without genuine faithfulness is worthless. The temple was full of activity but empty of purpose. The fig tree was full of leaves but empty of fruit. God isn't impressed by the appearance of devotion. He's looking for the real thing.

Third, rejecting God's messengers has consequences. The parables in this section are warnings, not threats from a bully. They're invitations to change course before it's too late. God is patient, but his patience has a purpose: repentance. When people refuse that purpose, judgment follows.

Fourth, love is the foundation of everything. When Jesus summarizes the entire Old Testament in two commands, he isn't reducing God's law to a bumper sticker. He's revealing its heartbeat. Love for God and love for neighbor aren't items on a checklist. They're the root system from which every other command grows.

TALKING POINTS

1. **The crowds praised Jesus but didn't really understand who he was.** What's the difference between being excited about Jesus and truly following him?

2. **Jesus drove the merchants out of the temple because it had lost its true purpose.** What are some ways churches today could lose sight of their purpose?

3. **In the parable of the two sons, one said yes but didn't go, and one said no but eventually went.** Which do you think you're more like, and why?

4. Jesus said to give Caesar what is Caesar's and God what is God's. What are some things that belong to God that people sometimes try to keep for themselves?

5. Jesus said the two greatest commandments are to love God and love your neighbor. How are those two connected? Can you have one without the other?

The king has arrived. He's been tested by every group with power in Jerusalem, and he's silenced them all. But the silence won't last. His enemies are gathering in the shadows, finalizing plans that have been forming since chapter 12.

Jesus knows it. He's known it since the beginning. And he's still walking forward, because the cross isn't a detour. It's the destination. It's the reason the king came to Jerusalem in the first place.

Turn the page.

11

WARNINGS, TEARS, AND THE END OF THE WORLD

Have you ever watched one of those reality TV shows where a health inspector walks into a restaurant? From the outside, the place looks fine. Nice sign. Clean front counter. Friendly staff. But once the inspector goes into the kitchen, everything falls apart. Grease everywhere. Expired food in the fridge. Mold in corners nobody cleaned. The restaurant looked great to the customers, but behind the scenes it was a disaster.

That's basically what happens in Matthew 23. Jesus walks into the religious "kitchen" of Jerusalem and exposes what's been hiding behind the polished exterior. He's done debating. He's done answering trick questions. Now he speaks directly to the crowds and his disciples, and what comes out of his mouth is the fiercest, most emotionally charged speech in the entire Gospel.

But the warnings don't stop there. After his blistering words about the religious leaders, Jesus leaves the temple for the last time and delivers his final teaching to the disciples. In chapters 24–25, he looks into the future and describes the destruction of the temple, the end of the age, and the final judgment. These are some of the most intense chapters in the Bible. They're also some of the most important, because they answer a question every generation asks: How should we live while we're waiting for Jesus to come back?

THE SEVEN WOES

Jesus begins by acknowledging that the scribes and Pharisees sit in Moses' seat, meaning they hold the official position of interpreting God's law. He tells the crowds to listen to what they teach but not to imitate what they do. Because they don't practice what they preach. They load heavy burdens of religious rules onto other people's shoulders but won't lift a finger to help carry them.

Then Jesus lists their problems. Everything they do is done for show. They wear extra-wide prayer boxes and extra-long tassels on their clothing so people will notice how religious they are. They love the best seats at banquets and the most important positions in the synagogues. They love being greeted with fancy titles in the marketplace.

Jesus tells his followers not to be like that. Don't seek honorary titles. Don't let people call you "Teacher" or "Father" as if you're above everyone else. You're all brothers and sisters. You have one Teacher, one Father in heaven, one Leader, and that's the Christ. The greatest among you will be your servant. Whoever exalts himself will be humbled, and whoever humbles himself will be exalted.

Then come the woes. Seven of them. In the Old Testament, a "woe" was a prophet's anguished cry of warning, part anger and part grief. Jesus uses the same form, and each woe targets a different way the religious leaders had corrupted their role.

They shut the door of the kingdom in people's faces, refusing to enter themselves and blocking others who try. They make converts and then turn those converts into worse hypocrites than themselves. They create elaborate systems for deciding which oaths are binding and which can be broken, as if you can trick God with fine print. They tithe tiny herbs from their gardens while ignoring justice, mercy, and faithfulness, the things that actually matter most. Jesus calls this straining out a gnat but swallowing a camel. They clean the outside of the cup but leave the inside filthy with greed and self-indulgence. They're like whitewashed tombs: beautiful on the outside, full of decay on the inside. And they build monuments to honor dead prophets while plotting to kill the living one standing right in front of them.

This isn't Jesus losing his temper. It's Jesus doing exactly what the prophets before him did. Jeremiah, Isaiah, and Amos all confronted religious leaders who used their position to benefit themselves instead of serving God's people. Jesus stands in that same tradition, and his anger is fueled by love, love for the people being misled and love for the leaders who are destroying themselves without knowing it.

JERUSALEM, JERUSALEM

Then the tone shifts dramatically. After all that fire, Jesus' voice breaks. "Jerusalem, Jerusalem, you who kill the prophets and stone those sent to you, how often I have wanted to gather your children together, as a hen gathers her chicks under her wings, and you were not willing."

This is one of the most heartbreaking moments in the Gospel. Jesus is not a cold judge pronouncing a verdict. He's a grieving king watching his own people choose destruction. The image of a mother hen sheltering her chicks under her wings comes from the Old Testament, where God himself is described as protecting Israel under his wings. Jesus is claiming that role and mourning the fact that Jerusalem has refused his protection.

He then declares that their house, meaning the temple, will be left desolate. They will not see him again until they say, "Blessed is the one who comes in the name of the Lord." Judgment is coming. But even in the middle of that announcement, there's a sliver of future hope.

WHEN WILL THE TEMPLE FALL?

As Jesus and the disciples leave the temple, the disciples point out the magnificent buildings. The temple complex covered roughly thirteen acres and was one of the most impressive structures in the Roman world. Jesus' response is stunning: not one stone here will be left on another. Every one will be thrown down.

Later, sitting on the Mount of Olives overlooking the temple, the disciples ask two questions: When will this happen? And what will be the sign of your coming and the end of the age? Jesus' answer weaves together the near future (the destruction of the temple in AD 70) and the distant future (his return at the end of history). This blending of near and far events was common in Old Testament prophecy, where a prophet might describe a coming invasion and the final day of the Lord in the same breath.

Jesus warns first about what won't signal the end. False messiahs will appear. Wars and rumors of wars will spread. Famines and earthquakes will strike. But these are just the beginning of birth pains, not the end itself. Many people throughout history have tried to use current events to predict when Jesus would return. Jesus says the opposite: don't be fooled by dramatic events into thinking the end is here.

What will happen before the end is persecution and betrayal. Christians will be hated by all nations. Some will fall away from the faith. Wickedness will increase, and the love of many will grow cold. But the one who stands firm to the end will be saved. And this gospel of the kingdom will be preached in the whole world as a testimony to all nations, and then the end will come.

That's the one clear marker Jesus gives for the end of the age: the gospel reaching all peoples. Not a political event. Not a natural disaster. The completion of the mission he's about to give his followers.

GREAT TRIBULATION AND THE RETURN

Jesus then warns about a specific event called the "abomination of desolation," borrowing language from the prophet Daniel. In Daniel's day, this phrase described a pagan ruler who desecrated God's temple. Jesus warns that something similar will happen again, and when it does, people in Judea should flee to the mountains without looking back. The suffering will be worse than anything the world has seen.

For Matthew's original readers, this prophecy was deeply personal. The Roman army destroyed Jerusalem and the temple in AD 70, and early church historians record that Jewish Christians in Jerusalem remembered Jesus' warning and fled the city before the destruction came.

But Jesus is also looking beyond that event to the end of history. False messiahs and false prophets will perform impressive signs. Don't follow them. When the Son of Man actually returns, it won't be subtle. It will be like lightning flashing from east to west. The sun will go dark. The moon will stop shining. The stars will fall. And the Son of Man will appear in the sky with power and great glory, sending his angels to gather his chosen people from every corner of the earth.

The return of Jesus is not a secret event. It's the most public, unmistakable moment in all of history.

BE READY: FOUR PARABLES

After describing the future, Jesus tells a series of parables that all drive home the same point: since you don't know when I'm coming back, you'd better be ready.

The Fig Tree and the Flood. Jesus compares the signs of the end to a fig tree putting out leaves, which tells you summer is near. But just as no one knew the exact day the flood would come in Noah's time, no one knows the exact day of Jesus' return. Not even the angels. Not even the Son. Only the Father. So stay alert. Two men will be working in a field; one will be taken and the other left. Two women will be grinding at a mill; one taken, the other left. Keep watch, because you don't know what day your Lord is coming.

The Faithful and Unfaithful Servants. A master puts a servant in charge of his household while he's away. If the servant does his job faithfully, the master will reward him with even more responsibility. But if the servant thinks the master is delayed and starts mistreating the other servants and partying, the master will come on a day the servant doesn't expect and will cut him off. This parable is a direct warning to leaders in the church. Those entrusted with caring for God's people will be held accountable for how they used that trust.

The Ten Bridesmaids. Ten young women take their lamps to meet a bridegroom coming for a wedding procession at night. Five bring extra oil. Five don't. When the groom is delayed and finally arrives at midnight, the five without oil scramble to buy more and arrive at the banquet hall to find the door locked. The groom says, "I don't know you." The lesson is blunt. You can't borrow someone else's readiness. Preparation for meeting Jesus is personal. You either have it or you don't, and you won't get a second chance to prepare after he arrives.

The Talents. A master going on a journey entrusts his money to three servants: five talents to one, two to another, and one to the last. (A single talent was worth roughly twenty years' wages for an ordinary worker, so even the servant with one talent received a fortune.) The first two servants invest and double their money. The third buries his in the ground. When the master returns, he praises the first two with the same words: "Well done, good and faithful servant. You have been faithful with a few things; I will put you in charge of many things. Come and share your master's happiness." But the third servant makes excuses about being afraid. The master calls him wicked and lazy and throws him out. God gives every person gifts, resources, and opportunities. He expects us to use them. Playing it safe because you're afraid isn't faithfulness. It's disobedience.

The Sheep and the Goats. This final parable is the climax of Jesus' entire public teaching ministry, and it's terrifying in its simplicity. The Son of Man comes in glory, sits on his throne, and separates all the nations like a shepherd separating sheep from goats. To the sheep on his right he says: I was hungry and you fed me, thirsty and you gave me drink, a stranger and you welcomed me, naked and you clothed me, sick and you visited me, in prison and you came to see me. The righteous are confused: when did we do any of that for you? The king answers: "Whatever you did for one of the least of these brothers and sisters of mine, you did for me."

To the goats on his left, he says the opposite. They didn't feed him, welcome him, clothe him, or visit him. They're equally confused. And the king says: whatever you did not do for one of the least of these, you did not do for me.

In context, the "least of these brothers and sisters" most likely refers to Jesus' followers, especially those who suffer for the sake of the gospel. The nations are being judged based on how they received or rejected the messengers Jesus sent into the world. To welcome a hungry, sick, imprisoned follower of Jesus is to welcome Jesus himself. To ignore them is to ignore him. The stakes are eternal.

WHAT THIS MEANS FOR US

First, religion without integrity is worse than no religion at all. The Pharisees knew the right words but lived the wrong lives. Jesus reserves his harshest words not for open sinners but for people who use God's name to build their own reputation.

Second, the future belongs to God, not to those who try to predict it. Jesus told his followers not to be tricked by false prophets or current events. Instead, he told them to be faithful, watchful, and busy doing what he commanded.

Third, readiness for Jesus' return isn't about having the right end-times chart on your wall. It's about living each day as if he could come back today: serving others, using what God gave you, caring for the vulnerable, and staying faithful even when the wait is long.

Fourth, how you treat the people nobody notices is how you treat Jesus. The sheep and goats parable makes that unmistakably clear. The final exam isn't about how much theology you know. It's about what you did with the opportunities God placed in your path.

TALKING POINTS

1. **Jesus said the Pharisees cleaned the outside of the cup but left the inside dirty.** What are some ways people your age might look "good" on the outside while ignoring what's happening inside?

2. **After seven fierce warnings against the religious leaders, Jesus' tone shifted to grief.** Why do you think Jesus wept over Jerusalem even after pronouncing judgment on its leaders? What does that tell you about God's heart?

3. **Jesus said no one knows the day or hour of his return.** Why do you think some people are so eager to predict it anyway?

4. **In the parable of the talents, the third servant buried his money because he was afraid.** Have you ever avoided using a gift or opportunity because you were scared of failing?

5. The sheep and goats parable says that serving "the least of these" is serving Jesus. Who are the "least of these" in your school, neighborhood, or community?

The debates are over. The teaching is done. Jesus has said everything he came to say. What happens next will be the most important three days in the history of the world. The king who rode in on a donkey, who wept over his city, who warned and pleaded and told stories and healed the broken, is about to walk into the darkest night any human has ever faced. And he's going to do it on purpose.

Turn the page.

12

THE DARKEST NIGHT AND THE BRIGHTEST MORNING

In the movie *The Princess Bride*, there's a scene where the hero, Westley, is captured and dragged into the Pit of Despair. Everything looks finished. The villain has won. The princess is lost. The audience knows the story isn't over yet, but if you were living inside that story, with no guarantee of a happy ending, you'd have every reason to give up.

That's what Matthew 26–28 feels like from the inside. The hero is betrayed by a friend. Abandoned by his closest followers. Arrested in the middle of the night. Put through two sham trials. Beaten. Mocked. Nailed to a Roman cross. Buried in a borrowed tomb.

If you had been standing there watching, you would have thought the story was over. The religious leaders certainly thought so. The Roman soldiers thought so. Even most of the disciples thought so.

They were all wrong.

These final three chapters of Matthew are the turning point of all human history. Everything the Gospel has been building toward, from the angel's announcement to Joseph, to the sermons and miracles and parables and warnings, all of it crashes together in the most devastating and most glorious weekend the world has ever known.

BETRAYAL AND A LAST MEAL

As Passover approaches, Jesus tells his disciples plainly: in two days the Son of Man will be handed over to be crucified. While he says this, the chief priests and elders are meeting at the palace of the high priest, Caiaphas, plotting how to arrest Jesus secretly and kill him. They just don't want to do it during the festival, because they're afraid of a riot.

Meanwhile, a woman in the home of a man named Simon the Leper pours an incredibly expensive bottle of perfume over Jesus' head. The disciples are angry. "This could have been sold and the money given to the poor!" But Jesus defends her. She has done a beautiful thing, he says, preparing his body for burial. Wherever the gospel is preached in the whole world, people will tell what she did.

The contrast between this woman and what happens next is staggering. Immediately after her act of extravagant love, Judas Iscariot goes to the chief priests and asks, "What are you willing to give me if I deliver him over to you?" They offer thirty pieces of silver, the Old Testament price of a slave. The woman gave everything she had to honor Jesus. Judas sold Jesus for pocket change.

At the Passover meal, Jesus drops a bomb: one of the twelve will betray him. The disciples are devastated. "Surely not I, Lord?" they ask, one after another. Jesus identifies the betrayer without exposing him to the group. Then, with Judas still in the room, Jesus does something extraordinary. He takes the bread, gives thanks, breaks it, and says: this is my body. He takes the cup and says: this is my blood of the covenant, poured out for many for the forgiveness of sins.

Passover had always been about remembering how God rescued Israel from slavery in Egypt. Jesus is redefining it. The bread and the cup now point to a new rescue, a new exodus. This time the lamb being sacrificed isn't an animal. It's the king himself.

GETHSEMANE: THE GARDEN OF AGONY

After the meal, Jesus takes the disciples to a garden called Gethsemane on the Mount of Olives. He tells them to sit while he goes ahead to pray. He takes Peter, James, and John further in, and then something happens that should break every reader's heart. Jesus tells them, "My soul is overwhelmed with sorrow to the point of death." He falls to the ground and prays: "My Father, if it is possible, let this cup be taken from me. Yet not as I will, but as you will."

The cup isn't just about physical pain, though that would be terrible enough. In the Old Testament, the "cup" was an image for God's judgment against sin. Jesus was about to drink the full weight of that judgment on behalf of the world. He was fully human, and as a human being he felt the full horror of what was coming. He didn't want it. He asked if there was another way. But he chose to obey.

Three times he prays. Three times he comes back and finds the disciples asleep. They couldn't even stay awake for one hour. Jesus' words to Peter are haunting: "Watch and pray so that you will not fall into temptation. The spirit is willing, but the flesh is weak." Within hours, those words would prove painfully true.

Then Judas arrives with a crowd armed with swords and clubs, sent by the chief priests. He greets Jesus with a kiss, the standard sign of respect between a student and a teacher. But this kiss is a signal to the soldiers. One of the disciples draws a sword and cuts off the ear of the high priest's servant. Jesus stops him: those who live by the sword die by the sword. He could call twelve legions of angels to rescue him. But then how would God's plan be fulfilled?

The disciples flee into the darkness. Every single one of them.

TWO TRIALS, TWO FAILURES

Jesus is dragged before the Sanhedrin, the Jewish ruling council, for a nighttime hearing that breaks nearly every rule of their own legal procedure. They bring in false witnesses, but the witnesses can't get their stories straight. Finally the high priest demands a direct answer: are you the Christ, the Son of the Blessed One?

Jesus answers yes. And he goes further: from now on, they will see the Son of Man sitting at the right hand of Power and coming on the clouds of heaven. The high priest tears his robes and calls it blasphemy. They spit in Jesus' face and hit him with their fists. They blindfold him and slap him, taunting, "Prophesy to us, Christ! Who hit you?"

The irony cuts deep. At the very moment they mock Jesus as a false prophet, his prophecy about Peter is being fulfilled in the courtyard below. A servant girl recognizes Peter, and he denies knowing Jesus. A second time, he denies it. A third time, with curses, he swears, "I don't know the man!" Then a rooster crows. Peter remembers Jesus' prediction from just hours earlier, goes outside, and weeps bitterly.

Judas, too, realizes what he has done. He tries to return the thirty pieces of silver to the chief priests. "I have sinned," he says. "I have betrayed innocent blood." They shrug. "What is that to us? That's your responsibility." Judas throws the money into the temple and goes out and hangs himself.

Two disciples. Two failures. But the difference matters. Peter's failure leads to tears and eventually to restoration. Judas's failure leads to despair and death. When we fail, and we will, the question is never whether Jesus will take us back. The question is whether we'll let him.

In the morning, the leaders bring Jesus before Pontius Pilate, the Roman governor, because only Rome can authorize a crucifixion. The charge is now political: Jesus claims to be a king. Pilate can see that the leaders have brought Jesus out of jealousy, not justice. His own wife sends him a message: "Don't have anything to do with that innocent man. I've suffered terribly in a dream because of him."

Pilate offers the crowd a choice: release Jesus or release Barabbas, an imprisoned rebel. The chief priests stir the crowd to demand Barabbas. Pilate washes his hands in front of them and says, "I am innocent of this man's blood." It changes nothing. You can't wash off responsibility by performing a ritual. Pilate orders Jesus to be flogged and handed over for crucifixion.

THE CROSS

The Roman soldiers strip Jesus and dress him in a scarlet robe. They twist together a crown of thorns and jam it on his head. They put a staff in his hand and kneel before him in mockery: "Hail, King of the Jews!" They spit on him and beat him with the staff. Then they strip the robe off and lead him out to be crucified.

On the way, they force a bystander named Simon from Cyrene to carry the crossbeam. The disciples who had promised to follow Jesus to the death are nowhere to be found. A stranger does what they wouldn't.

At a place called Golgotha ("the place of the skull"), they nail Jesus to the cross. They post the charge above his head: THIS IS JESUS, THE KING OF THE JEWS. The soldiers divide his clothes among themselves. Passersby hurl insults. The religious leaders mock him: "He saved others but he can't save himself! Let him come down from the cross and we'll believe!"

Matthew's readers would catch the terrible irony. They're right, in a way they don't understand. He can't save himself and save others. If he comes down from the cross, nobody gets saved. The whole point of his mission is that he stays.

From noon until three in the afternoon, darkness covers the land. Then Jesus cries out in the words of Psalm 22: "My God, my God, why have you forsaken me?" It's not a loss of faith. The psalm begins in agony but ends in triumph. But in this moment, Jesus is experiencing the full weight of separation from his Father, taking on the sin of the world so that we would never have to face that separation ourselves.

Jesus cries out again with a loud voice and gives up his spirit.

Then everything shakes. The curtain of the temple tears in two from top to bottom. The earth quakes. Rocks split. Tombs break open. The curtain that had separated ordinary people from the most holy place in the temple, symbolizing the barrier between God and humanity, is ripped apart. Not from the bottom up, as if a person did it. From the top down. God did it.

The Roman centurion standing guard at the cross watches all of this and says, "Surely he was the Son of God!" The pagan soldier gets it. The religious leaders never did.

BURIED AND GUARDED

A wealthy man named Joseph of Arimathea, who had become a disciple of Jesus, goes to Pilate and asks for the body. He wraps it in clean linen, places it in his own new tomb cut into the rock, rolls a large stone across the entrance, and leaves. Mary Magdalene and the other Mary sit there watching.

The next day, the chief priests and Pharisees go to Pilate and ask for a guard to be posted at the tomb. They're worried the disciples might steal the body and claim a resurrection. Pilate agrees. They seal the stone and post soldiers.

They think they've sealed the story shut. They haven't even come close.

THE MORNING EVERYTHING CHANGED

At dawn on the first day of the week, Mary Magdalene and the other Mary go to the tomb. There is a violent earthquake. An angel descends from heaven, rolls back the stone, and sits on it. His appearance is like lightning. His clothes are white as snow. The guards are so terrified they shake and collapse.

The angel speaks to the women: "Do not be afraid, for I know that you are looking for Jesus, who was crucified. He is not here; he has risen, just as he said."

Just as he said. He told them this would happen. He told them in chapter 16. He told them in chapter 17. He told them in chapter 20. And now it has happened, exactly as he promised.

The women run from the tomb, afraid and filled with joy. And then Jesus himself meets them on the road. They grab his feet and worship him. He is real. He is physical. He is alive.

Meanwhile, the guards report to the chief priests, who bribe them to spread a lie: tell people the disciples stole the body while you were sleeping. Think about that for a moment. Sleeping witnesses are, by definition, not witnesses. The story is absurd on its face. But the lie spreads anyway.

The eleven remaining disciples travel to a mountain in Galilee where Jesus told them to go. When they see him, they worship, though some still doubt. Even seeing the risen Jesus doesn't automatically produce perfect faith. Belief is a choice, not just a response to evidence.

Then Jesus speaks the words that have sent his followers to every corner of the earth for two thousand years: "All authority in heaven and on earth has been given to me. Therefore go and make disciples of all nations, baptizing them in the name of the Father and of the Son and of the Holy Spirit, and teaching them to obey everything I have commanded you. And surely I am with you always, to the very end of the age."

That's how Matthew ends. No ascension scene. No dramatic goodbye. Just a command and a promise. The command: go and make disciples of every nation. The promise: I am with you. Always.

The Gospel opened with the name Immanuel, which means "God with us." It closes with the same truth. The king who was born in Bethlehem, who taught on the mountain, who healed the sick, who calmed the storm, who welcomed the outcast, who confronted the hypocrites, who wept over Jerusalem, who died on a Roman cross, and who walked out of a sealed tomb, that king is still here. He's not a memory. He's not a philosophy. He's a living presence who promises never to leave.

WHAT THIS MEANS FOR US

First, everyone in this story fails except Jesus. The disciples run. Peter denies. Judas betrays. Pilate caves. The crowd chooses Barabbas. Only Jesus stays faithful, all the way to the end. The gospel isn't a story about strong people following a good teacher. It's a story about weak people being rescued by a faithful king.

Second, the cross is not a tragedy that God managed to fix. It's the plan. Jesus chose it. The Father ordained it. The Scriptures predicted it. From the very first chapter, Matthew has been building toward this moment. The cross is where Jesus' kingship is most fully revealed, because this is a king who conquers by dying for his enemies.

Third, the resurrection is the foundation of everything. Without it, Jesus is just another dead teacher with inspiring ideas. With it, he is exactly who he claimed to be: the Son of God, the King of kings, the Lord of life and death. The empty tomb is the reason the church exists.

Fourth, the Great Commission is not optional. Jesus doesn't say "go if you feel like it." He says go. Make disciples. Teach. Baptize. And he backs the command with the greatest promise in Scripture: I am with you always.

TALKING POINTS

1. **The woman with the perfume gave her most valuable possession to honor Jesus. Judas sold Jesus for the price of a slave.** What does the contrast between these two actions teach us about what it means to follow Jesus?

2. **In Gethsemane, Jesus asked if there was another way, but then said "not my will, but yours."** Have you ever had to do something hard because you knew it was right, even though you didn't want to?

3. **Peter denied Jesus three times but was later restored.** Judas betrayed Jesus and took his own life. What made the difference between their two responses to failure?

4. **The Roman centurion at the cross, a pagan soldier, recognized Jesus as the Son of God while the religious leaders missed it completely.** Why do you think that happened?

5. **The Great Commission tells us to "go and make disciples of all nations."** What does that look like for someone your age, in your school and neighborhood?

The tomb is empty. The king is alive. And the story isn't over. It's just beginning.